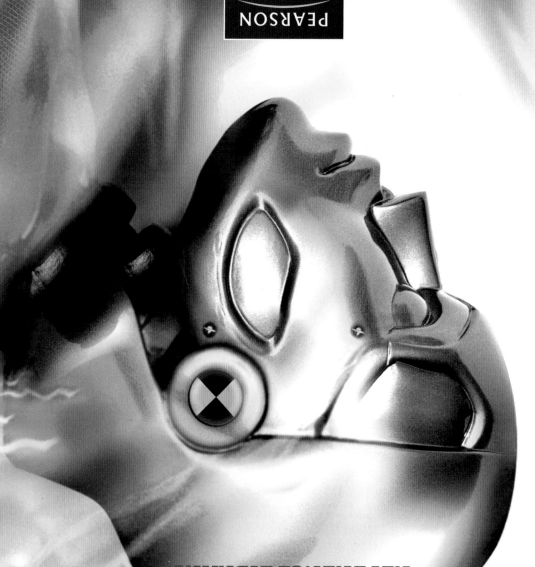

BIG
IDEAS
OF SCIENCE
REFERENCE LIBRARY

DK

BIG
IDEAS
OF SCIENCE
REFERENCE LIBRARY

PEARSON

Boston, Massachusetts
Chandler, Arizona
Glenview, Illinois
Upper Saddle River, New Jersey

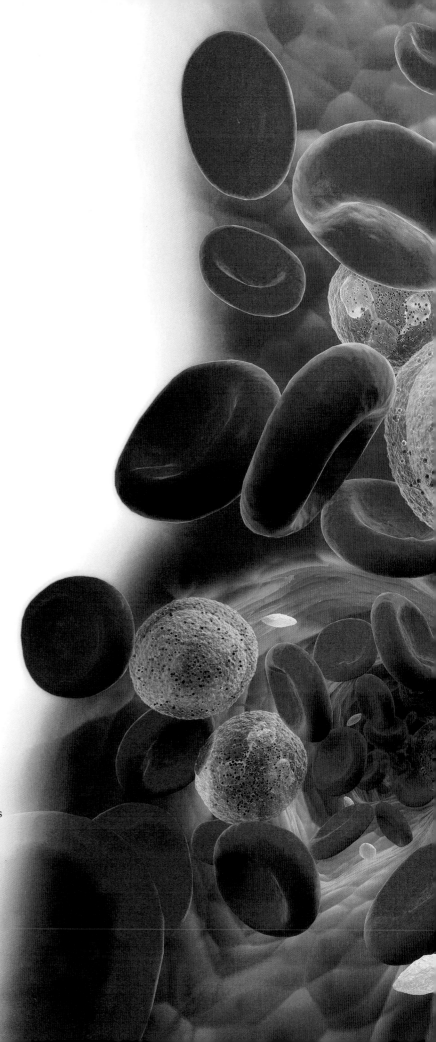

ISBN-13: 978-0-13-369868-8
ISBN-10: 0-13-369868-8

5 6 7 8 9 10   V057   14 13 12

CONTENTS

KEY
These symbols appear in the top right corner below the topic name
to connect the topic to the branches of science.

Earth Science   Life Science   ⊛ Physical Science

BIG IDEAS OF EARTH SCIENCE 🌍

The Big Ideas of earth science help us understand our changing planet, its long history, and its place in the universe. Earth scientists study Earth and the forces that change its surface and interior.

Earth is part of a system of objects that orbit the sun.

Asteroids
Astronomy Myths
Bay of Fundy
Comets
Constellations
Earth
Gravity
Jupiter's Moons
Mars
Mars Rover
Mercury
Meteorites
Moon
Neptune
Pluto
Saturn
Solar Eclipse
Solar Power
Space Probes
Summer Solstice
Uranus
Venus

Earth is 4.6 billion years old and the rock record contains its history.

Atmosphere
Dating Rocks
Deep Sea Vents
Dinosaurs
Eryops
Extinction
Family Tree
Fossils
Geologic Time
Giant Mammals
Ice Age

Earth's land, water, air, and life form a system.

Altitude
Atacama Desert
Atmosphere
Aurora Borealis
Buoys
Doppler Radar
Dust Storms
Earth's Core
Floods
Fog
Gliding
Predicting Hurricanes
Rainbows
Sailing
Snowmaking
Storm Chasing
Thunderstorms
Weather Fronts

Earth is the water planet.

Amazon River
Beaches
Drinking Water
Everglades
Great Lakes
Mid-Ocean Ridge
Niagara Falls
Ocean Currents
Sea Stacks
Surfing
Thermal Imaging
Tsunami
Upwelling
Water

Earth is a continually changing planet.

Acid Rain
Afar Triangle
Caves
Coal

Colorado Plateau
Colorado River
Coral Reefs
Crystals
Dunes
Earthquakes
Equator
Fluorescent Minerals
Geocaching
Geodes
Geysers
Glaciers
Gold Mining
Hoodoos
Ice Age
Islands
Kilauea
Landslides
Lava
Mapping
Marble Quarries
Mid-Ocean Ridge
Mount Everest
Niagara Falls
Rain Forest
Rubies
Sea Stacks
Soil
Terrace Farming
Tour de France
Tsunami

Human activities can change Earth's land, water, air, and life.

Air Pollution
Energy Conservation
Equator
Fuel Cell Cars
Global Warming
Ice Age
Ocean Currents
Rain Forest
Shelter

The universe is very old, very large, and constantly changing.

Big Bang Theory
Black Holes
Constellations
Hubble Space Telescope
Milky Way
Quasars
Universe

Science, technology, and society affect each other.

Astronauts
Hubble Space Telescope
Jetpacks
International Space Station
Mars Rover
Predicting Hurricanes
Robots
Satellite Dish
Science at Work
Space Technology
Space Tourism
Virtual World

Scientists use mathematics in many ways.

Buoys
Doppler Radar
Mars Rover
Measurement
Neptune

Scientists use scientific inquiry to explain the natural world.

Extinction
Predicting Hurricanes
Wind Power
Neptune

BIG IDEAS OF LIFE SCIENCE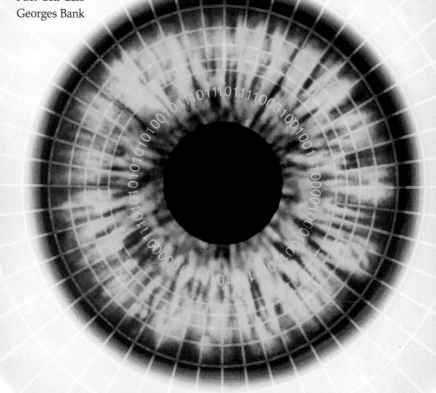

Life scientists study organisms, their life processes, and how they interact with one another and their environment. The Big Ideas of life science help us understand how living things are organized, how they get and use energy, and how they reproduce.

Living things grow, change, and reproduce during their lifetimes.

Animal Communication
Bush Baby
Courtship Rituals
Echolocation
Gorillas
Hummingbirds
Hypothalamus
Instinct
Marsupials
Menstrual Cycle
Penguins
Pregnancy
Puberty
Sea Horse
Seals
Sleep
Sloth
Tasmanian Devil
Twins
Worms

Living things are made of cells.

Blood Types
Cactus
Cell Division
Microscopes
Quarks and Leptons
Scent Pollution
Skeletons

Living things are alike yet different.

Adaptations
Aerogels
Bacteria
Bats
Bears
Cactus
Common Cold
DNA Connections
Exoskeleton
Family Tree
Farming
Ferns
Flowers
Frankenfoods
Fungi
Geckos
Giant Mammals
Gila Monster
Insects
Jellyfish
Naming
Patterns in Nature
Plant Tricks
Rain Forest
Red Tide
Redwoods
Scent Pollution
Skeletons
Snakes
Soil
Spiders
Survival
Symmetry
Taco Science
Whales

Living things interact with their environment.

Acid Rain
Air Pollution
Amazon River
Atacama Desert
Bats
Bay of Fundy
Beaches
Biodiversity
Biofuels
Bush Baby
Butterflies
Camouflage
Coal
Colorado Plateau
Deep Sea Vents
Energy Conservation
Everglades
Farming
Forestry
Frozen Zoo
Fuel Cell Cars
Georges Bank

Global Warming
GPS Tracking
Great Lakes
Hybrid Vehicles
Insects
Islands
Kilauea
Light Bulbs
Mid-Ocean Ridge
Mount Everest
Oil Spills
Patterns in Nature
Plant Invasion
Plastic
Population Growth
Rain Forest
Recycling
Red Tide
Renewal
Sea Horse
Seaweed
Seed Bank
Sharks
Shelter
Skywalk

Sloth
Soil
Solar Power
Supercooling Frogs
Sushi
Upwelling
Vultures

Genetic information passes from parents to offspring.

Blood Types
Colorblindness
DNA Evidence
Frankenfoods
Frozen Zoo
Genetic Disorders
Human Genome Project
Hummingbirds
Mutations
Probability

Living things get and use energy.

Algae
Barracuda
Birds
Cell Division
Elephants
Hummingbirds
New Body Parts
Octopus
Scorpion
Sea Horse
Seals
Sour Milk
Tasmanian Devil
Teeth

Structures in living things are related to their functions.

ACL Tear
Aerobic Exercise
ALS
Altitude
Animal Bodies
Birds
Blood Pressure
Blood Types
Brain Power
Broken Bones
Defibrillators
Digestion
Dolphins
Drinking Water
Exoskeleton
Fats

Gliding
Hearing Loss
Heartbeat
Hummingbirds
Jellyfish
Kidney Transplant
Laser Eye Surgery
Left vs. Right Brain
Marsupials
No Smoking
Open-Heart Surgery
Prosthetic Limb
Scent Pollution
Sea Turtles
Simulators
Singing
Skeletons
Skin
Sleep
Sloth
Steroids
Superfoods
Teeth
The Bends
Tour de France
Tweeters and Woofers
Vitamins and Minerals
Weightlifting

Living things change over time.

DNA Connections
Family Tree
Gorillas
Islands
Madagascar
Racehorses

Living things maintain constant conditions inside their bodies.

Allergies
Astronauts
Cancer Treatment
Common Cold
HIV/AIDS
Malaria
Marathon Training
Mold
MRI
Pandemic
Rats
Rheumatoid Arthritis
Scent Pollution
Sleep
Thermal Imaging
Vaccines
Working Body

Scientists use mathematics in many ways.

Census
Estimation
Hazardous Materials
Measurement
Probability
Simulators

Science, technology, and society affect each other.

Biomimetics
Clinical Trials
DNA Evidence
Eye Scan
Human Genome Project
Prosthetic Limb
Robots
Science at Work
Truth in Advertising

Scientists use scientific inquiry to explain the natural world.

BPA
Crittercam
Forensics
Human Genome Project
Naming
Quarks and Leptons
Truth in Advertising

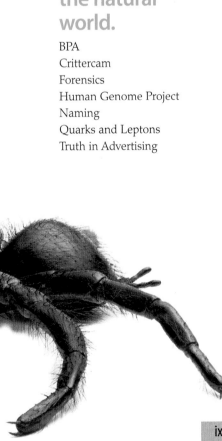

BIG IDEAS OF PHYSICAL SCIENCE

Physical scientists study matter and energy. The Big Ideas of physical science help us describe the objects we see around us and understand their properties, motions, and interactions.

A net force causes an object's motion to change.

Asteroids
Astronauts
Bridges
Collision
Crew
Drag Racing
Formula 1 Car
Gravitron
Gravity
Hockey
Hovercraft
Jetpacks
Meteorites
Quasars
Roller Coaster
Sailing
Skydiving
Snowboard
Tour de France

Energy can take different forms but is always conserved.

Aerogels
ALS
Aurora Borealis
Bicycles
Black Holes
Bridges
Bungee Jumping
Catapults
Cordless Drill
Crew
Defibrillators
Earth's Core
Energy Conservation
Geocaching
Gliding
Headphones
Hoover Dam
Hybrid Vehicles
Lichtenberg Figures
Lifting Electromagnets
Light Bulbs
Microscopes
MP3 Player
MRI
Niagara Falls
Radio
Roller Coaster
Rube Goldberg Devices
Skyscraper
Skywalk
Submarines
Taco Science
Thermal Imaging
Weightlifting

Waves transmit energy.

Animal Communication
Cellphone
Color
Digital Camera
Doppler Radar
Echolocation
Eye Scan
Fluorescent Minerals
Geocaching
GPS Tracking
Guitar
Headphones
Hearing Loss
Holograms
Hubble Space Telescope
Hummingbirds
Laser Eye Surgery
Lighthouse
Microscopes
Mirages
Night Vision Goggles
Predicting Hurricanes
Radio
Rainbows
Rubies
Satellite Dish
Sea Stacks
Seaweed
Singing
Solar Power
Sonic Booms
Surfing
Thunderstorms
Tsunami
Tweeters and Woofers
Virtual World

Atoms are the building blocks of matter.

Acid Rain
Black Holes
Body Protection
Caves
Creating Elements
Crystals
Geckos
Glass
Gold Mining
Mars Rover
Melting Point
Meteorites
Nuclear Medicine
Prosthetic Limb
Quarks and Leptons
Steel
The Bends
Water

Mass and energy are conserved during physical and chemical changes.

Digestion
Earth
Fire Extinguishers
Fireworks
Forestry
Hovercraft
Ice Houses
Lava
Melting Point
Scent Pollution
Snowmaking
Supercooling Frogs
The Bends

Scientists use mathematics in many ways.

Buoys
Hazardous Materials
Mars Rover
Measurement
Wind Tunnel

Scientists use scientific inquiry to explain the natural world.

Biomimetics
Forensics
Quarks and Leptons
Wind Power

Science, technology, and society affect each other.

Bridges
Cellphone
Formula 1 Car
Hubble Space
    Telescope
Light Bulbs
Prosthetic Limb
Robots
Science at Work

CAVES

No, there was not an explosion at the vanilla pudding factory. These drips and blobs are solid rock inside a cave. Caves can form in several ways—boulders move apart, surf wears away rock, or lava hardens into a tube. But most caves form the way this one did—from water seeping into rock and dissolving it. Rain mixing with carbon dioxide in the air forms a watery acid that can dissolve minerals in rocks. This solution flows underground through cracks and small spaces between rocks. Over time, it dissolves minerals in one place and deposits them in another, creating and reshaping these underground hollows.

Stalactites

Stalagmites

Pools of water

▲ HARRISON'S CAVE
The many passages and rooms of Harrison's Cave, on the Caribbean island of Barbados, stretch over at least 1.4 miles (about 2.25 km). The largest room has ceilings that are nearly 50 feet (15 m) high. Like most caves formed by dissolving rocks, this one is made of limestone.

◄ ICICLES AND DRIP CASTLES
Mineral formations called *stalactites* extend like delicate soda straws from the ceiling of a cave and grow in much the same way as icicles. Often, where the mineral-containing water drips down from the stalactite, a second kind of formation, called a *stalagmite*, grows upward from the cave floor, like a sandcastle made by dripping watery sand. Eventually, these two formations can grow together and form a column.

This close-up of a stalactite shows how a mineral solution drips down from it.

▲ LIMESTONE CAVES

The mineral in limestone that is dissolved when caves form is called *calcite*. It is the chalky remains of organisms such as clams and corals that were deposited in ancient oceans. Landscapes that include hollows from dissolved rock, such as in many parts of Florida, are known as *karsts*.

did you know? IT CAN TAKE MORE THAN 100 YEARS FOR A STALACTITE TO GROW JUST HALF AN INCH!

CELL DIVISION

A person, an elephant, and a snake look very different from one another. Yet all three begin life as a single cell. So how does that cell become an adult elephant, with trillions of cells? It all starts with cell division. The first cell splits into two cells, two cells split into four, four cells split into eight, and so on. After three days, the cluster of cells, called the elephant *embryo,* consists of approximately 30 cells—called *embryonic stem cells.* These stem cells have the amazing ability to become any type of cell in the body—blood cells, brain cells, heart muscle cells, bone cells, or even hair cells in the inner ear! As the elephant's stem cells continue to divide, they become the different types of cells that together make an elephant.

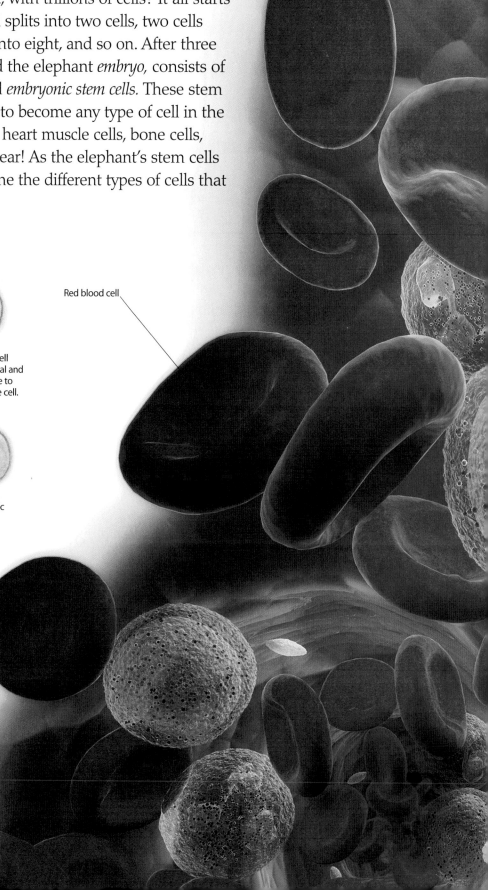

Red blood cell

Before a cell splits, it makes a copy of its genetic information, or DNA.

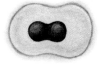

The nucleus of the cell splits, and the original and duplicate DNA move to opposite ends of the cell.

A cell membrane begins to form around each nucleus as the cell pulls apart.

Each new cell now has one copy of the genetic information.

▲ SPLITTING UP

Cell division helps organisms grow larger—from a single cell into a 12,000-pound (5,443-kg) adult elephant, for example. Cells also divide to repair and replace parts of the body. The cells on the edge of a cut divide to form new skin. Dead skin cells are constantly being replaced by newly divided cells. Some other adult cells, such as nerve cells, do not divide as often.

◄ WHAT KIND OF CELL WILL I BE?

Once an elephant—or a person— becomes an adult, it has fewer stem cells. It does have some, though, called *adult stem cells.* In the bone marrow, for example, stem cells keep dividing to replace old cells. These stem cells can become red or white blood cells or platelets, each of which has a different job. The organism's DNA and signals throughout the body determine what type of cell each stem cell should become.

A lymphocyte, a type of white blood cell, targets infections and cancers.

did you know? ....
STEM CELLS IN AN AVERAGE ADULT'S BONE MARROW GENERATE ABOUT 610 BILLION BLOOD CELLS PER DAY!

Inner hair cells transmit signals to the brain.

Outer hair cells receive vibrations.

Nerve fiber

This platelet will clump with other platelets to help blood clot when we cut ourselves.

White blood cells destroy harmful foreign organisms. This neutrophil, the most common type of white blood cell, targets harmful bacteria.

HAIR FOR HEARING ▲

Inside a mammal's inner ear is a chamber, called the *cochlea,* where sensory cells, called *hair cells* because of their tiny hairlike projections, help transmit sound. Damage to these hairs causes hearing loss. Researchers are exploring ways to grow stem cells that may generate new hair cells.

CELLPHONE

Running late? No problem—pull out your cellphone and make a call. What did we ever do without cellphones? Because they use radio signals instead of wires, they can go wherever we go—hiking, driving, even boating. Your cellphone sends out a radio signal, which is picked up by a cell tower within range. Each tower serves an area, called a *cell,* and each cell has many assigned channels, used by many phones. Using the newest technology, digital phones convert voice signals into code. The code is compressed, sent by radio signal, and then decompressed on the other end. Of course, cellphones only work if you keep the battery charged, stay in range of a tower, and don't put your phone through the laundry! So, send a text message, make a call, and enjoy the technology of cellphones!

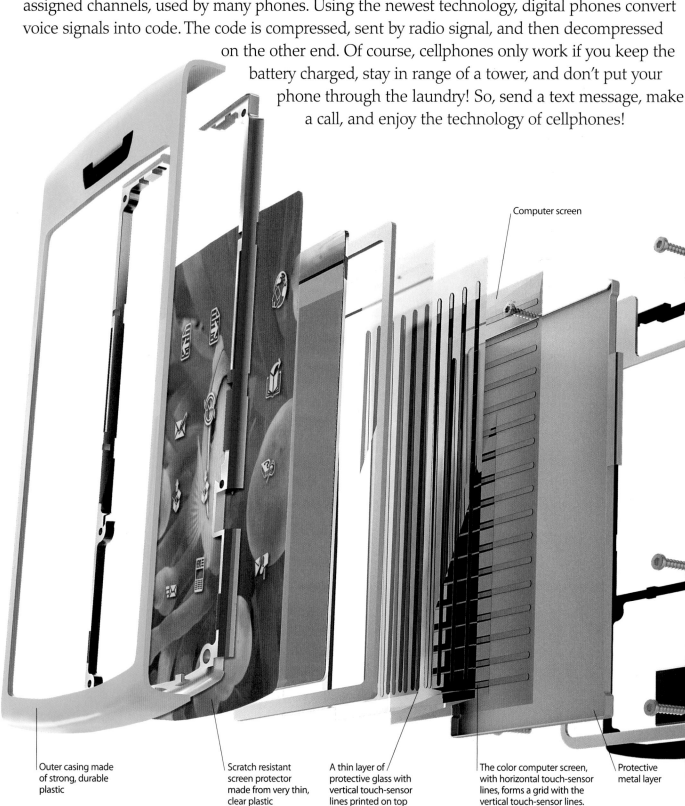

Computer screen

Outer casing made of strong, durable plastic

Scratch resistant screen protector made from very thin, clear plastic

A thin layer of protective glass with vertical touch-sensor lines printed on top

The color computer screen, with horizontal touch-sensor lines, forms a grid with the vertical touch-sensor lines. A touch can then be located on the grid.

Protective metal layer

CAN YOU HEAR ME? ▶

What will this communications satellite do once it's launched into orbit? It will transmit television signals, Internet signals, cellphone signals, and more. Though most cellphones use towers to transmit signals, calls that go around the world use satellites to pick up and transmit their signals. Satellites can transmit signals in remote areas where cell towers have not been installed.

did you know?
U.S. CELLPHONE USERS SEND OR RECEIVE ON AVERAGE 357 TEXT MESSAGES PER MONTH. TEENS AVERAGE 1,742 MESSAGES.

LOTS AND LOTS OF LAYERS ▼

The touch screen of a cellphone has many layers, each with a special purpose. At the base is a computer screen, which is divided into a grid of pixels, or tiny squares. Individual pixels light up to create the words and images we see. On top of the screen is a touch-sensitive grid. Other layers create space to protect the touch screens from damage, dirt, and moisture.

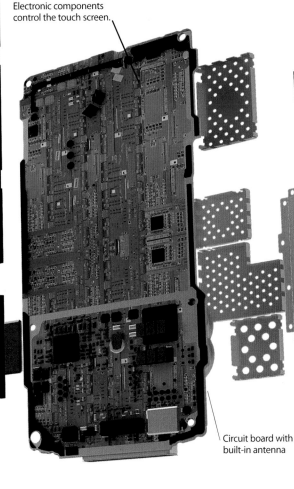

Electronic components control the touch screen.

Circuit board with built-in antenna

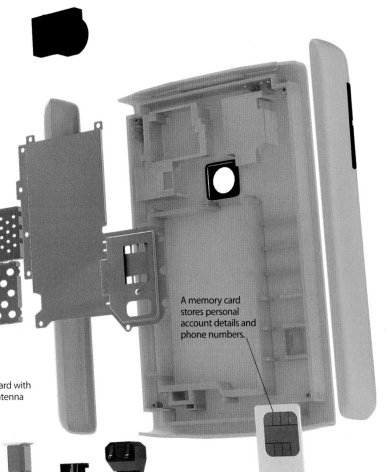

A memory card stores personal account details and phone numbers.

CENSUS

How many people on Earth are more than 100 years old? What foods do most people in Bangladesh eat? How many bald eagles are there in Alaska? Believe it or not, a census could answer all of these questions and more. A census is a collection of information about a population—human or otherwise. It can show a population's growth and change. It shows characteristics such as age, race, income level, and education—collectively called *demographics.* Census data can reveal trends. A local politician may study the demographics of her district to help plan a reelection strategy. A scientist might study environmental factors affecting bald eagles' eggs to understand a decrease in population. A census is a powerful tool.

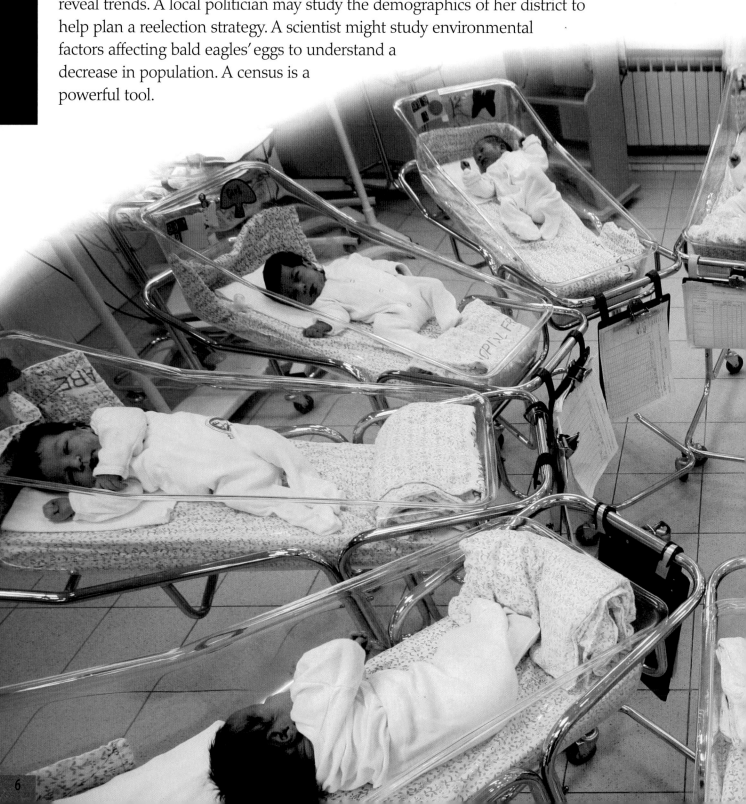

NEWBORNS APLENTY ▼

Some communities have declining populations. But the world's population is increasing, because babies are born at a faster rate than the death rate. Population growth and demographics are valuable statistics measured by the census. Governments, scientists, and engineers use this information to plan resources for growing populations. How much food storage does each city need? Which places need new power supplies to meet a growing population?

AGING AROUND THE WORLD ▲

The world map shows the percentage of each country's population that is age 65 or older. Blue stands for less than five percent; yellow, 5–9 percent; gold, 10–14 percent; and red, 15 percent or greater. You can see that, on average, people tend to live longer in Europe and Japan. Yet few live to be 65 in Africa and some other areas. This information helps people and scientists of all nations focus on areas of the world that still need aid to promote survival. Graphing this type of data from different years can show population trends.

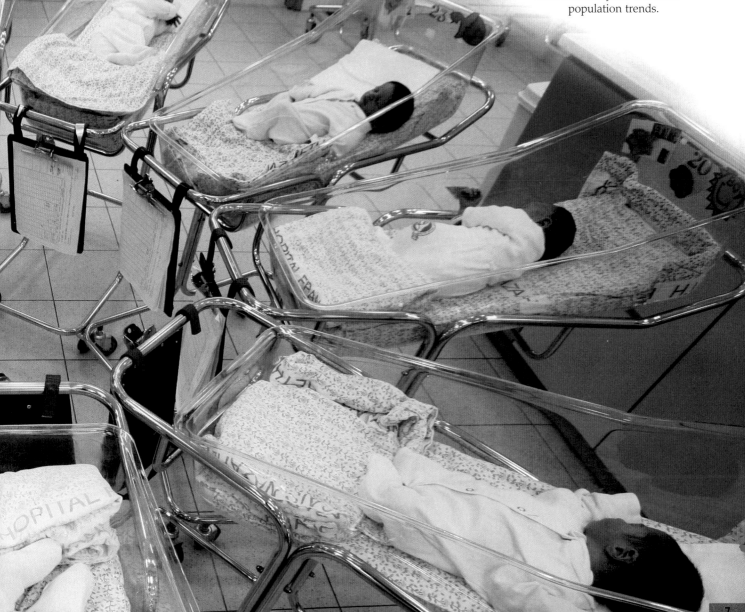

CLINICAL TRIALS

Have you taken medicine recently for an illness? How do you know it's safe—and whether it actually works? In the past, draining blood from a patient was a common remedy for many illnesses. Doctors once thought tobacco could cure asthma and bad breath! Why did people believe such unscientific nonsense? One reason is that until the early 1960s, doctors did not use scientific methods to evaluate medical treatments. Now doctors rely on carefully designed research studies called *clinical trials.* In a clinical trial, people volunteer to test new drugs, medical devices, or procedures, to help researchers see if they are safe and effective. Clinical trials help doctors figure out whether new treatments work—or whether they work better than the treatments that are already available.

◄ FROM THE LAB TO THE PATIENT

Clinical trials are the last step in the long process of developing a new medication. Before a drug is tested in clinical trials, scientists have already done lots of laboratory research, including testing the drug on different types of cells and on animals. Most drugs don't make it past this stage, as most of their laboratory tests are unsuccessful. In fact, only one in a thousand drugs is considered promising enough to move on to clinical trials.

Petri dishes hold a gel used for growing cells in the laboratory.

WHAT DO CLINICAL TRIALS TEST?

Thousands of clinical trials are conducted every year. Some test new drugs, such as cancer medicine. Others test new medical devices, such as a new type of heart monitor. Clinical trials also test new methods of surgery or new ways of diagnosing a disease. Some even test the health effects of different foods.

HOW DO CLINICAL TRIALS WORK?

Clinical trials are conducted in a series of steps called *phases*. In a Phase I trial of a drug, researchers test the drug on a small group of healthy people to learn what dose is safe and what the side effects are. In a Phase II trial, researchers test the drug on a larger group of volunteers who have the disease the medicine is meant to treat.

Each volunteer signs an informed consent form that explains the possible risks and benefits of the drug.

AVOIDING BIAS

If the new drug seems effective and safe during Phase II, then it moves on to a Phase III trial. Now it is given to a larger group of people who have the disease. A computer randomly divides them into two groups. One group gets the new drug. The other group gets either the standard treatment or an inactive medicine, called a *placebo*. Most clinical trials are double-blind. This means that neither the participants nor the researchers know who is getting the new drug. If they knew, it might affect their view of the drug's effectiveness or side effects. Double-blind trials help prevent bias—anything that might affect the results of the study.

COAL

Did you know that you can use dead plants to turn on your lights? Well, kind of. Some electricity in the United States is produced by coal, which, at its basic level, is made from dead plants—really dead ones—millions of years old. When layer upon layer of plant remains are compressed under rocks and dirt for millions of years, the result is coal—a brownish-black sedimentary rock that burns. Coal is made up of carbons and hydrocarbons, which are quite combustible. The energy that was trapped in the plants underneath all the rocks and soil is released when the coal is burned. Power plants burn coal to make steam, and the steam turns turbines that produce electricity. So dead plants = working light bulbs.

did you know? U.S. COAL DEPOSITS CONTAIN MORE ENERGY THAN ALL THE OIL IN THE WORLD.

SURFACE MINING ▼

When coal is buried less than 200 feet (about 61 m) underground, it can be surface mined. Most of the coal in the United States is mined this way. Monstrous machines remove the topsoil and expose the coal beds beneath. After the coal is mined, the topsoil is replaced. This coal mine is in Wyoming—where about 40 percent of the nation's coal is mined.

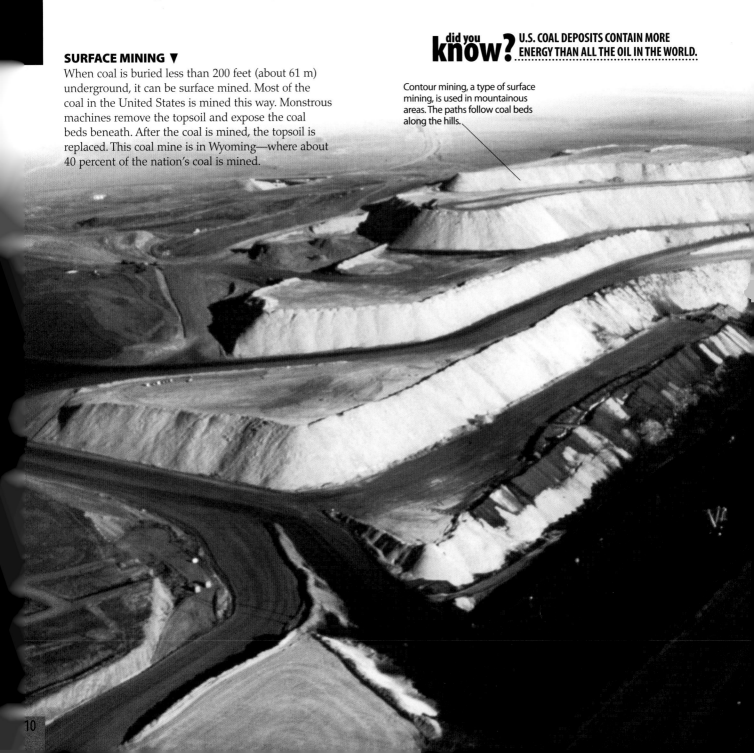

Contour mining, a type of surface mining, is used in mountainous areas. The paths follow coal beds along the hills.

HOW COAL FORMED ▼

Coal is a fossil fuel, made from the remains of ancient animals and plants. Coal is also a nonrenewable resource. Once it is used up, it cannot be replenished.

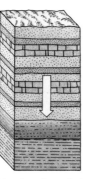

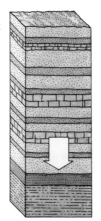

From 100 to 300 million years ago, giant plants containing lots of energy lived in swampy forests.

The giant plants died and were buried. As they decayed, they formed a material called *peat*.

Over millions of years, the pressure exerted by accumulated sediments and heat compressed the peat into different types of coal such as lignite, anthracite, subbituminous, and bituminous coal.

The coal bed is divided up and mined in layers.

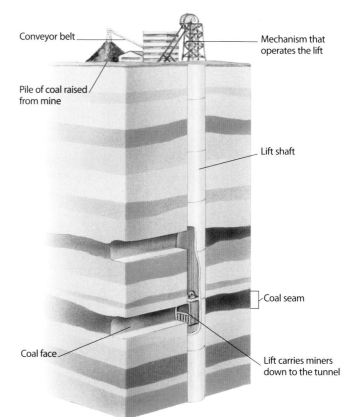

Conveyor belt

Mechanism that operates the lift

Pile of coal raised from mine

Lift shaft

Coal seam

Coal face

Lift carries miners down to the tunnel

DEEP MINING ▲

Coal is sometimes buried more than 200 feet (61 m) underground. Brave miners take elevators down deep mine shafts. They cut the coal from the coal face with huge machinery and send it up on long conveyor belts.

COLLISION

The pitch and . . . the swing. There's a sudden, loud crack and the ball soars toward the fence. This is the kind of collision you hope for when you're playing baseball. Both the ball and the bat are moving, so they have what is called *momentum.* Momentum equals the mass of an object times its velocity. Velocity is speed with direction. During a hit, some of the bat's momentum is transferred to the ball. Since the mass of the ball does not change, this momentum goes into changing the ball's velocity. Instead of moving toward home plate, the ball is now soaring toward the right field fence. The total momentum of the bat and ball is conserved—that is, the total is the same before and after the collision. So the bat's momentum must decrease by the same amount as the ball's momentum increases by. So what's the secret to hitting a home run? Transfer enough momentum to hit the ball out of the park.

HEROIC DUMMIES ▶

A car crash is called an *inelastic collision.* When cars collide, they don't bounce off one another. Instead, metal crunches and bends, glass breaks, and sound waves carry energy away. Human bodies are not designed to absorb these sudden changes in energy and momentum. Crash test dummies are built to find out what happens to people in a car crash. Scientists use the information to design systems to protect passengers.

did you know? ....
MANY SCIENTISTS BELIEVE THAT THE MOON FORMED AFTER A COLLISION BETWEEN EARTH AND A MARS-SIZED ASTEROID BILLIONS OF YEARS AGO.

ELASTIC BUMPERS ▲

In what is called an *elastic collision,* the colliding objects bounce off of each other and don't change shape. All of the energy goes into changes in speed. Bumper boats are a great way to feel an elastic collision. As your boat smacks into your friend's boat, you both go spinning away from the collision.

Crash test dummies come in many sizes and shapes— adult men and women, children, infants, and even pregnant women.

Airbag

Joints are designed to move as human joints do.

The airbag fills with gas in a fraction of a second—faster than the blink of an eye.

As the airbag inflates, the seat belt locks in place, so that the dummy—or a person—does not keep moving forward as the car stops.

FALLING INTO A BALLOON ▲

If a car stops suddenly, the people in it will keep moving until something stops them. The soft surface of an airbag stops a person more slowly than either the dashboard or steering wheel. This results in less force on the person.

COLOR

Why is an orange orange and a blueberry blue? The things we see have a spectacular array of colors because of visible light. Light travels in waves. Light waves have different distances between the peaks of their waves. This distance is called a *wavelength.* You see different wavelengths as different colors. Together, all of these colors make up white light. But when light hits an object, some colors are absorbed and others are reflected. An object takes on the color it reflects. So we see a blueberry as blue because it reflects light with a blue wavelength.

VIOLET

Violet is the name given to the light with the shortest wavelength. *Purple* is the name given to the color you get when you mix blue and red pigments.

THE VISIBLE LIGHT SPECTRUM

The colors that the human eye can see make up what's called the *visible light spectrum.* This range includes every color in the rainbow. Red light has the longest wavelength. As you move counterclockwise around this color wheel from red, wavelengths decrease.

ORANGE AND YELLOW

Pigments are molecules that give things color by absorbing some colors and reflecting others. Carrots and bananas, for example, contain a pigment called carotene, which absorbs all colors of light except for orange and yellow.

DARK BLUE

The blue pigment known as *ultramarine* comes from blue semi-precious stones called *lapis lazuli.* Renaissance painters often saved this precious pigment to color only the most important people in their paintings.

did you know?

THE PIGMENT CALLED *ANTHOCYANIN* MAKES EGGPLANTS LOOK PURPLE AND GIVES BLUEBERRIES THEIR COLOR.

IRIDESCENT BLUE

The blue morpho butterfly's color is not caused by a pigment. Tiny ridges on its wings cause the wings to reflect the blue wavelength of light. The wings seem to sparkle as the light bounces at different angles. This effect is called *iridescence.*

GREEN

The pigment that makes plants green is called *chlorophyll.* Chlorophyll absorbs all colors of light except green. When leaves change color in the fall, it is because the chlorophyll has begun to break down, and the other pigments in the leaves can be seen. These pigments reflect red, orange, and yellow light.

COLORADO PLATEAU

When you think of the southwestern United States, you probably picture the red, striped landscape of the Colorado Plateau. The region includes 130,000 square miles (about 337,000 sq km) surrounding the point where the corners of Utah, Colorado, New Mexico, and Arizona meet. A plateau is a high, flat-topped expanse of land with steep sides. Although it looks like a chopped off mountain, it's really a rock that rose up. The Colorado Plateau formed 10 million years ago when a large, flat piece of layered rock began to rise, as squeezing forces deep in Earth's crust pushed it upward. Such a rise in a large mass of land is called *uplifting*, a process that also gave us the Rocky Mountains. Water cut into the steep sides of the plateau, and wind began to slowly tear it down. Over millions of years, water and wind erosion has carved many of the beautiful landforms we know today.

◄ **POUNCING**
The diverse landscape of the Colorado Plateau makes it home to a wide variety of animals, including bobcats. Bobcats are about twice the size of a house cat. They have soft, spotted brown fur, a white belly, and a short tail with a black tip. They live alone and hunt small animals, such as birds, rabbits, and other small mammals.

SWOOPING ▶

One of the largest raptors (birds of prey) in North America is the golden eagle. Found in the western United States and Mexico, it tends to nest up high in trees or on the ledges of steep cliffs. The golden eagle benefits from the diversity of wildlife in the plateau region, eating mostly small mammals, such as rabbits and squirrels. It surveys its prey from the air and then, using its powerful wings, swoops down from above, catching its next meal off guard.

did you know?
A PLATEAU IS SOMETIMES CALLED A *TABLELAND*, BECAUSE IT HAS THE SAME SHAPE AS A TABLE

A golden eagle gets ready to land by spreading its feathers and reaching out with its sharp talons.

This raptor has a wingspan of six and a half feet (almost 2 m).

The flat-topped edge on either side of a canyon is called a *rim*.

The worn-away rock face reveals layers of rock. Each layer comes from a different moment in geologic time.

◀ CARVING THE PLATEAU

Water has made a jigsaw puzzle of the plateau. Canyons form as rivers slowly erode layers of rock, creating a steep-sided groove in the earth. The Grand Canyon, in the Arizona portion of the Colorado Plateau, has a vertical drop of 6,000 feet (almost 1,829 m) at its deepest point.

COLORADO RIVER

The Colorado River stretches 1,450 miles (about 2,334 km). From its source in Colorado's Rocky Mountains, the river flows to the Gulf of California in Mexico. It drains an area of 244,000 square miles (almost 632,000 sq km), which makes up almost one-twelfth of the area of the United States (minus Alaska and Hawaii). The river carries precious water through some of the driest parts of North America. People use the river for drinking water, transportation, water sports, and food. It provides a source of fresh water for crops. It also drives hydroelectric power plants, such as the one at the base of Hoover Dam. The river and its banks are home to many different kinds of wildlife. River otters, beavers, coyotes, bats, rattlesnakes, red-spotted toads, catfish, and bass are only a few of the animals that depend on the river for food, water, and shelter.

Each thin layer of rock in the cliff wall represents a relatively narrow band of time in Earth's long history.

did you know? RAFTING THE COLORADO RIVER IS SO POPULAR THAT THE NATIONAL PARK SERVICE HOLDS A LOTTERY FOR TRIP PERMITS EACH YEAR.

▼ SWIM, RATTLE, AND COIL

The western diamondback is a poisonous rattlesnake that thrives in dry areas, but can swim. They usually live in dens located in rocky outcroppings. These fierce predators can strike a victim who is as far away as two-thirds the snake's body length. That's pretty dangerous given that they can grow to more than 7 feet (2.1 m) long! They give fair warning with their rattling sound, which is made when hollow segments of the tail hit each other.

Every time the snake sheds its skin, it adds another hollow segment to its tail.

The diamondback gets its name from the dark pattern on its scaly back.

After striking and killing its prey, a rattlesnake will open its triangular jaws and swallow the meal whole.

▼ GEOLOGIC HISTORY IN THE CANYON WALLS

About 277 miles (446 km) of the Colorado River flow through the Grand Canyon. Exposed by erosion, the oldest rocks on these cliff faces are nearly 2 billion years old. The uncovered layers of rock and the fossils they contain make up one of the most complete geologic histories in the world. The oldest layers are at the bottom of the cliffs and the newest layers make up the canyon rims.

▼ EROSION BY A RIVER

A canyon forms over millions of years as water carried by a river washes away rock and soil bit by bit. This process, called *erosion,* cuts a steep groove into the earth. Due to the action of water, wind, and earthquakes, the Grand Canyon began forming 17 million years ago as two smaller canyons. They eventually broke through and met about 6 million years ago. In some places, the Grand Canyon is 1 mile (about 1 km) deep.

Erosion by wind and rain can cause an occasional landslide from the rocky face of the canyon.

The river carries away the eroded material, called *sediment,* and drops it downstream.

COLORBLINDNESS

Roses are red . . . or are they brown? How can you be sure the roses you see look the same to other people? What if you see colors differently? You wouldn't be alone, especially if you are a male. As many as 1 in 12 men has a color vision problem. The condition is called *colorblindness,* even though only a small percentage of people cannot see any color at all. The most common form of colorblindness is called *red-green colorblindness.* People who have it can't distinguish between red and green—both colors look sort of yellow or brown to them. This type of colorblindness is inherited, and most frequently passes from mother to son.

did you know?..................
TYPICALLY THE HUMAN EYE CAN SEE THOUSANDS—SOME SAY MILLIONS—OF COLORS.

▲ **WHEN GREEN + RED = YELLOW**
People who have red-green colorblindness cannot see a big color difference between this red postman butterfly and the green plant. Such inherited characteristics, or *traits,* are determined by the coded instructions, called *genes,* a person receives from each parent. A change, or *mutation,* of a gene causes red-green colorblindness. It is called a *sex-linked* trait, because it is passed to offspring in the same bundle of genes—called the *XY chromosomes*—that determines sex.

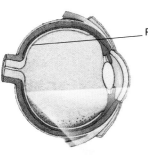

Retina

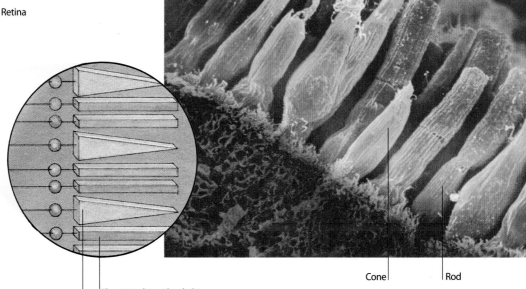

Cone | Rod

HOW DO WE SEE COLORS? ▲

The retina is a light-sensitive membrane at the back of the eye. It has three types of color-sensitive nerve cells called *cones*. Each type of cone is sensitive to either red, green, or blue light.

The retina has other light-sensitive cells called *rods* that function in dim light but don't react to colors.

The red, green, and blue cones work together so that the eye sees a full spectrum of colors.

WHAT CAUSES COLORBLINDNESS? ▲

Colorblindness occurs if one or more of the three types of cones is missing or defective. If the problem affects one type of cone, you have trouble seeing the difference between red and green—so the butterfly and leaf might look like the one below. If it affects two types, you also have trouble distinguishing between blue and yellow. If all three types of cones are missing, you can't see any colors.

Both the red on the butterfly's wings and the green leaves look yellowish.

WHY ARE MALES MORE LIKELY TO BE COLORBLIND?

The gene for colorblindness travels on the X chromosome. Everyone receives an X from his or her mother. From the father, a girl gets another X and a boy gets a Y. Even though girls have two Xs, they are rarely colorblind (fewer than 1 in 100). An X for normal vision masks the effect of a mutated one, but a Y cannot. If the one X that males get from their mother is carrying the mutated gene, they will be colorblind. A female has to receive *two* mutated Xs in order for the trait show up.

COMETS

Many years ago, people thought that comets signaled wars, plagues, and other catastrophes. In 1910, when Halley's comet appeared, some people bought gas masks because they were afraid that Earth would pass through the comet's tail. Today, however, we know that comets are nothing to be feared. They are harmless balls of ice and dust in orbit around the sun. When a comet's orbit brings it close to the sun, the frozen gases begin to evaporate. These evaporated gases and the dust particles they carry form a long tail behind the comet. We need a telescope to see most comets, but a few very bright ones can be seen from Earth with the naked eye. Some comets have predictable orbits that bring them near the sun every few years or every few hundred years. Others have such huge orbits that they pass only once in thousands of years.

COMET HALE BOPP

In 1995, two amateur astronomers, Alan Hale and Thomas Bopp, discovered one of the brightest comets ever seen from Earth. The comet, near Jupiter's rings, was one thousand times brighter than Halley's comet had been at the same distance. It was visible from Earth with the naked eye for 18 months—a new record. From Hubble Space Telescope's images, scientists estimated the comet's diameter to be about 25 miles (40 km).

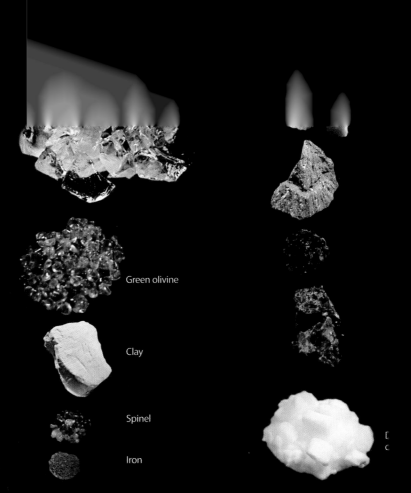

Green olivine

Clay

Spinel

Iron

INGREDIENTS OF A COMET ▲

The icy core of a comet is more than half frozen water an percent carbon. However, there are other substances in t ammonia, carbon dioxide, carbon monoxide, and methar few. Because comets have been largely unchanged since with the solar system 4.6 billion years ago, they offer gre what our planets were originally composed of.

Kuiper belt, icy matter that orbits the sun at a distance beyond Neptune

OORT CLOUD ▶

The Oort cloud is a huge spherical cloud that surrounds the outer edge of our solar system. It contains as many as a trillion icy bodies. When stars get close to the Oort cloud, their gravity can pull these icy bodies out of the Oort cloud and into our inner solar system. These bodies become comets, with large orbits that can take 30 million years to orbit our sun.

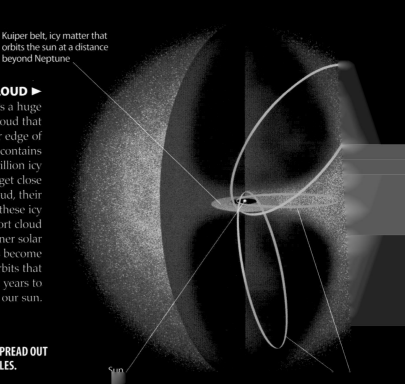

did you know? THE GASES IN A COMET'S TAIL CAN SPREAD OUT FOR HUNDREDS OF MILLIONS OF MILES.

Sun

COMMON COLD

"Ah…ah….ah…Achoo! Oh, do. I tink I hab a code!" You know it when you feel it: a headache, sore throat, stuffed up nose, sneezing, coughing, and the seemingly endless river of snot. You have a cold! More than 200 different viruses can cause the common cold. Because so many different germs are responsible for this familiar illness, scientists and doctors have little hope of finding an effective cure anytime soon. The easiest way to take care of a cold is to never catch it in the first place. Keep clear of uncovered sneezes, and wash your hands regularly. Soap and water will kill a cold virus, which can otherwise survive for hours on surfaces such as doorknobs, railings, drinking cups, money, and skin.

DAY 3: SORE THROAT AND MILD FEVER

The sore throat that you feel is not from the death of cells destroyed by the viruses. Instead, the discomfort comes from the immune system signals produced by your own body. They cause swelling of the tissues and trigger pain-sensing nerve cells. Other immune system signals cause fever and aching pain in your head and muscles.

THE STAGES OF A COLD ▶

A cold can last one to two weeks and may make you feel downright miserable. But while a virus is to blame for the infection, it is your body's immune response that causes the symptoms you have come to dread.

DAYS 1 & 2: INFECTION

You catch a cold when viruses enter your nose or throat and start to multiply using your own cells as tiny viral factories. But, who gave you those viruses? It's not always easy to tell. It takes two or three days for any cold symptoms to appear. You can spread viruses to others within a day of infection and for as many as three days after you no longer feel sick.

did you know? A SNEEZE CAN HAVE THE WIND SPEED OF A CATEGORY 2 HURRICANE. ....

DAYS 4 & 5: RUNNY NOSE AND SNEEZING

Mucous glands in your nose start making mucus, or snot, a slippery liquid that contains water and proteins. Snot may start out clear and colorless but soon becomes green due to the presence of a green coloring in white blood cells that are fighting your infection. Snot helps wash the viruses out of your body, and sneezing helps blast them out at a faster pace.

DAYS 6 & 7: STUFFINESS AND COUGHING

The stuffed up feeling that makes it hard to breathe is not from all the snot. It is due to the dilation of blood vessels in the nose tissues, also caused by immune system signals. When the infection gets far down into your throat, the irritated nerves cause coughing. Coughing can help move infected mucus that has built up in the lungs out of your body.

DAY 20: PROBABLY NOT A COLD

If you are sneezing for more than two weeks, see a doctor. A cold might not be your problem. An allergen like pollen is more likely to blame. Some sneezers mistake allergies for colds. Many of the symptoms are the same, but colds do not usually cause itchiness in the eyes and nose as allergies often do. Also, allergy symptoms do not usually include the achy fever and colorful snot that are signs of a cold.

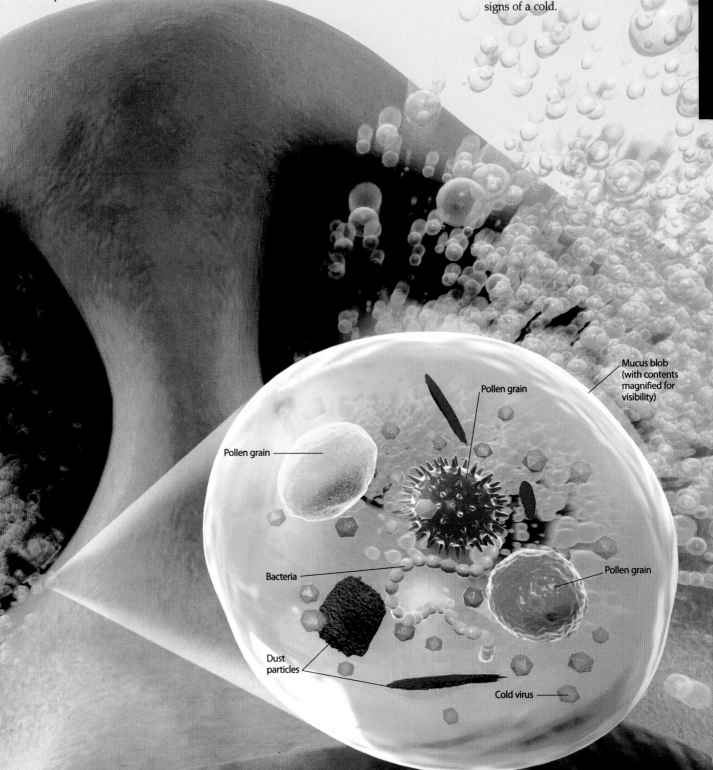

Pollen grain

Pollen grain

Mucus blob (with contents magnified for visibility)

Bacteria

Pollen grain

Dust particles

Cold virus

CONSTELLATIONS

Have you ever looked into the night sky and seen pictures in the stars? If so, you are in good company. Constellations came from the imaginations of people from ancient cultures who saw pictures in the stars. They gave these pictures names and stories based on the myths of their cultures. Constellations are groups of stars that form a pattern. In all, there are 88 recognized constellations in our sky, most of which were named by the Greeks and Romans. Because Earth spins and orbits the sun, the locations of constellations appear to change with the seasons. They also change depending on which hemisphere you are standing in. If you are down under in Australia, you can see the Southern Cross but not Draco, the dragon. Up north in Canada, you can see Draco but not the Southern Cross.

ORION, THE HUNTER ▶

According to Greek mythology, Orion was a mighty hunter with a big ego. In one story, he bragged that he could kill any animal. To punish Orion's arrogance, the Earth goddess Gaea sent Scorpius, the scorpion, to kill him. The Greeks honored Orion and Scorpius by setting them in the stars. According to the myth, they were placed on opposite sides of the sky so that Scorpio appears to be chasing Orion. Look at the stars below that form the Orion constellation.

❶ BETELGEUSE
Orion's right shoulder

❷ BELLATRIX
Orion's left shoulder

❸ ALNITAK, ALNILAM, AND MINTAKA
The three stars that form Orion's belt

❹ RIGEL
Orion's left leg or foot

❺ SAIPH
Orion's right leg or foot

❻ ORION NEBULA
Orion's sword, a giant cloud of gas and dust

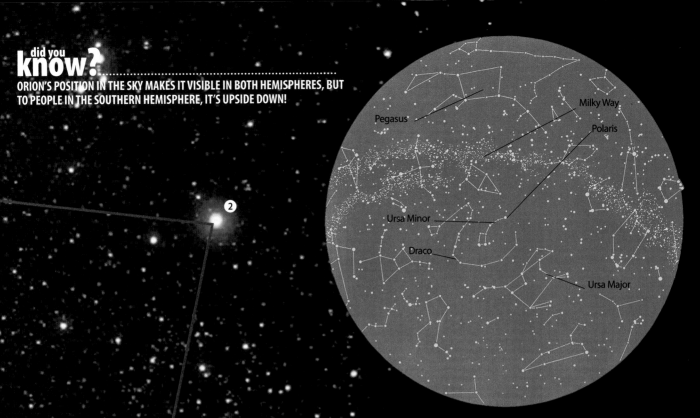

Pegasus
Milky Way
Polaris
Ursa Minor
Draco
Ursa Major

▲ NORTHERN HEMISPHERE CONSTELLATIONS

If you live in the Northern Hemisphere, look for Pegasus, the flying horse, and Ursa Minor, the little bear. At the tip of Ursa Minor's tail shines Polaris, the North Star, which lies almost directly above the North Pole. For thousands of years, Polaris has been used to aid in navigation. Sailors, nomads, and escaping slaves all depended on Polaris to find their way.

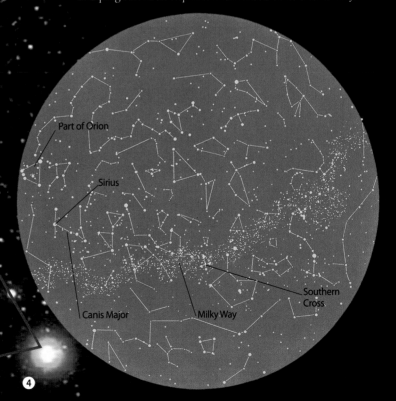

Part of Orion
Sirius
Canis Major
Milky Way
Southern Cross

▲ SOUTHERN HEMISPHERE CONSTELLATIONS

One of the most important constellations in the Southern Hemisphere is Canis Major—the greater dog— because it contains Sirius, the brightest star in the sky.

CORAL REEFS

Coral reefs are often called "rain forests of the oceans" because of the huge number of sea creatures that live there. The most essential inhabitant in a coral reef, however, is the coral. Reefs are formed by corals that live in groups, called *colonies*. A coral's body is a small, round, pouchlike sac called a *polyp*. The bottom of a polyp is attached to a surface, and the top consists of a mouth and tentacles. Some polyps are the size of a pinhead, while others are a foot (about 30 cm) wide. The coral polyp uses calcium from seawater to make a hard limestone cup to live in. After the coral dies, other corals build their homes on top of it. Millions of hard cups together form a coral reef.

Mount Otemanu rises in the center of the island.

▲ COLORFUL CORALS

Inside a coral polyp lives a special kind of one-celled algae. The algae use photosynthesis to make nutrients, which the coral shares. The coral, in turn, provides a safe place for the algae to live. These algae give corals their color. If the algae die, the corals turn white, a process called *coral bleaching*. Disease, pollution, and increased water temperature can all cause coral bleaching.

A SOUTH PACIFIC REEF ▶

This coral reef near the island of Bora Bora formed when coral larvae attached themselves to the submerged edges of an island volcano. Over time, the reef grew outward and upward and formed what is called an *atoll*, a ringed reef around the island. Atolls, along with other types of reefs, need warm water and sunlight to grow.

HOW CORAL REEFS FORM ▶

Coral reefs are formed from the skeletons of generation after generation of coral polyps. Most reefs are 5,000 to 10,000 years old. The sedimentary rock known as limestone can form from coral skeletons that are compacted to form rock. People use limestone to make cement and to neutralize acids.

did you know?........................

ALTHOUGH CORAL REEFS COVER ONLY 0.2 PERCENT OF THE OCEAN FLOOR, THEY CONTAIN MORE THAN 25 PERCENT OF ALL MARINE LIFE!

Layers of lava and ash have built up from volcanic eruptions.

Living corals grow at or near the surface.

Vegetation grows on top of nonliving coral skeletons.

Corals grow in water that is warm, salty, shallow, and clear.

An edge of the reef

An atoll is a circular ring of coral reef that surrounds a volcanic island.

CORDLESS DRILL

ZZWEEP! ZZWEEP! Drilling holes. NRRR . . . NRRR . . . Whoops, battery's dead! It takes energy to do work, and a cordless drill gets its energy from a rechargeable battery. Plugging in the battery to recharge it starts a series of energy conversions. Electrical energy from the plug flows into the the charger, and then it flows into the battery. Chemicals in the battery store the energy as electric potential, or voltage. All charged up! Pulling the trigger converts this potential energy back to electrical energy. This runs the motor, converting the electrical energy into kinetic energy—the energy of motion—to turn the drill bit. ZZWEEP! Back to work.

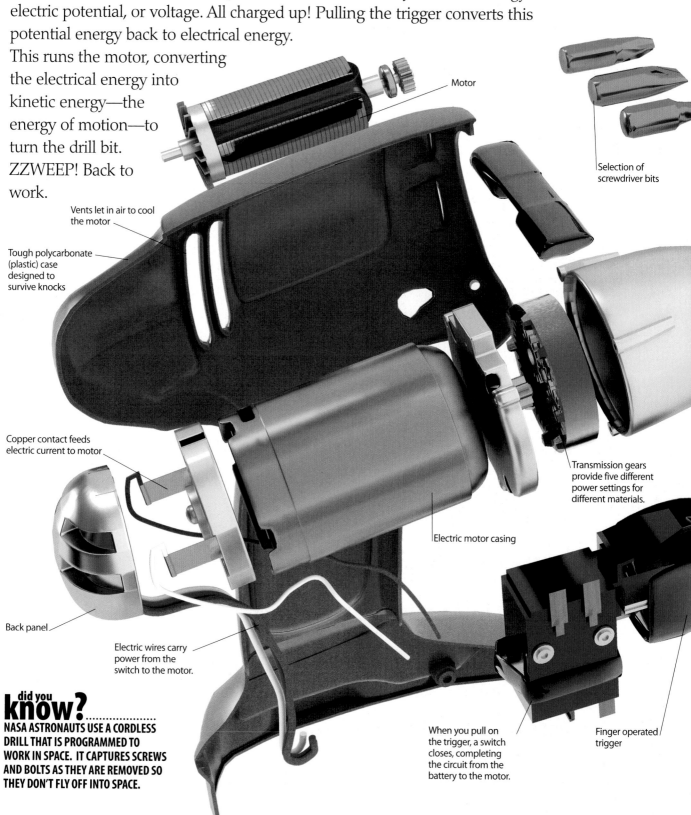

Motor

Selection of screwdriver bits

Vents let in air to cool the motor

Tough polycarbonate (plastic) case designed to survive knocks

Copper contact feeds electric current to motor

Transmission gears provide five different power settings for different materials.

Electric motor casing

Back panel

Electric wires carry power from the switch to the motor.

did you know?
NASA ASTRONAUTS USE A CORDLESS DRILL THAT IS PROGRAMMED TO WORK IN SPACE. IT CAPTURES SCREWS AND BOLTS AS THEY ARE REMOVED SO THEY DON'T FLY OFF INTO SPACE.

When you pull on the trigger, a switch closes, completing the circuit from the battery to the motor.

Finger operated trigger

SPEED! ▼

What makes a power tool powerful? Speed! Power is defined as the rate at which work is done. Power tools do most jobs faster than hand tools do. But different jobs require different speeds. Drills have gears like those on bicycles to adjust what's called the *torque,* or twisting force, applied to the bit. At slower speeds, the drill's power increases its torque, to drill through—or put a screw into—tough materials.

Selection of drill bits

Chuck holds drill and screwdriver bits tightly.

Screwdriver bit

Twist grip for tightening chuck

Connection between battery pack and base of drill

Grip adjusts the level of torque.

Wires connect the battery to the switch.

Battery inside battery pack

Outer case of battery pack

COURTSHIP RITUALS

When animals are looking for a mate, they have many different ways
of getting each other's attention. The term *courtship ritual* is used to
refer to the behavior that animals display before mating. The list of
things that animals do during courtship rituals is as long and
diverse as the number of different animals themselves.
Some of these rituals are fairly simple, while others
are more complex. They involve any or all of
the animals' senses. From simple mating
calls to elaborate dances, the main
goal of all animal courtship
rituals remains the same—
reproduction. Animals seek
out the best mates with
which to reproduce in
order to have healthy
offspring with the best
chance of survival.

Gannets mate for life—
and these birds can live
to be up to 40 years old.

BOWING AND PREENING ▶
Gannets bow to greet each other. This
is the beginning of their distinctive
courtship display. Then they point
their heads up and preen each other
(smooth each other's feathers). This
may seem more peculiar than human
behavior, but the goal is the same—to
show the bond between two creatures.

**did you
know?**............
YOUNG GANNETS "PLAY HOUSE" BY PRACTICING
BUILDING NESTS AND GOING THROUGH COURTSHIP
RITUALS BEFORE THEY ARE SEXUALLY MATURE.

UNCOMPLICATED GIRAFFES ▶

Giraffes have one of the more straightforward courtship rituals out there. A male tastes the urine of the female giraffe. This tells him whether she is in estrus (ready to mate and become pregnant). If she is, he'll mate with her. If not, he moves on.

A giraffe rubs the neck of another giraffe to show interest.

TAILS OR CALLS? ▲

Among male peacocks, looks are everything—or are they? Many people believe the elaborate tails that male peacocks display during courtship attract females. Other researchers have found that "male shivering displays," in which the males shake their tail feathers, attract females with a rustling noise. Finally, some studies show that neither the rustling noise nor the appearance of the tail is the main factor in mating success. They say the male's loud mating call is the main attractant.

CREATING ELEMENTS

Scientists describe the origin of the universe as a sudden expansion of matter and energy—the big bang. Particles formed, and then joined to create some of the elements. Three minutes after the big bang, most of the hydrogen that exists today had formed. It took a while longer to make helium and traces of lithium—maybe 35 minutes or so. The rest of the elements were formed in the stars. Elements are made in the stars through nuclear fusion, which is the formation of heavier elements from lighter ones. As a star burns its fuel, gravity pulls its material inward and it gets hotter—hundreds of millions of degrees hotter. Then, atoms collide and fuse to make the heavier elements. It takes the intense heat of supernovas to make elements heavier than iron. A supernova is an explosion of a huge star. The pieces flung out in this explosion come together to create new stars and planets. That's how elements that formed in the stars came to exist on Earth.

THE PERIODIC TABLE ▶

The periodic table is a tool that people use to organize the elements. Each element has a unique identity, determined by the number of protons in its nucleus—called its *atomic number*. Atomic numbers increase from left to right in each row. The elements in the same column have similar chemical and physical properties. The table shows each element's symbol, which is a one- or two-letter abbreviation.

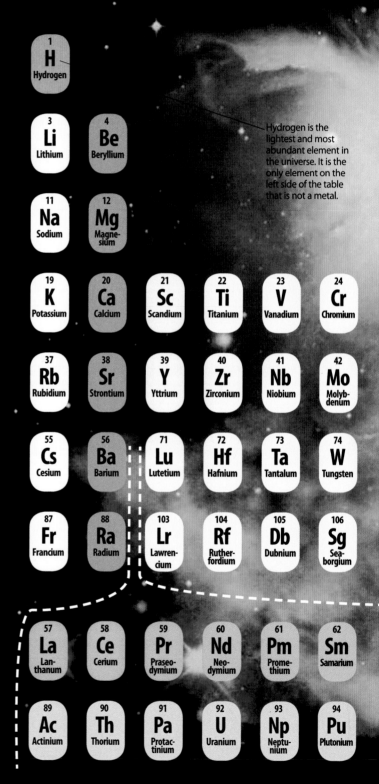

Hydrogen is the lightest and most abundant element in the universe. It is the only element on the left side of the table that is not a metal.

did you know? MORE THAN 40 ELEMENTS ARE FOUND IN THE HUMAN BODY, BUT CARBON, OXYGEN, HYDROGEN, AND NITROGEN MAKE UP 96 PERCENT OF OUR CELLS.

◄ BIRTHPLACE OF STARS

A supernova is essentially the death of a star. It blows the outer layers of a star far into space. Its matter mixes with interstellar gases, mostly hydrogen, forming a huge cloud of dust and gas called a *nebula*, like the one shown here. Within the nebula, gravity pulls bits and pieces together, forming new stars. Part of the material forms planets, such as Earth, whose core is mostly iron.

Along with hydrogen, elements shown in green and blue, to the right of the metalloids, are nonmetals. Their properties are very different from those of the metals.

					2 **He** Helium
5 **B** Boron	6 **C** Carbon	7 **N** Nitrogen	8 **O** Oxygen	9 **F** Fluorine	10 **Ne** Neon
13 **Al** Aluminum	14 **Si** Silicon	15 **P** Phos-phorus	16 **S** Sulfur	17 **Cl** Chlorine	18 **Ar** Argon

The metalloids (light green) share properties with metals and nonmetals.

Most of the elements are metals. There are 24 nonmetals and metalloids. All the other elements, from the left-most column (except hydrogen) to the elements shown in light blue, are metals.

25 **Mn** Manga-nese	26 **Fe** Iron	27 **Co** Cobalt	28 **Ni** Nickel	29 **Cu** Copper	30 **Zn** Zinc	31 **Ga** Gallium	32 **Ge** Germa-nium	33 **As** Arsenic	34 **Se** Selenium	35 **Br** Bromine	36 **Kr** Krypton
43 **Tc** Tech-netium	44 **Ru** Ruthe-nium	45 **Rh** Rhodium	46 **Pd** Palladium	47 **Ag** Silver	48 **Cd** Cadmium	49 **In** Indium	50 **Sn** Tin	51 **Sb** Antimony	52 **Te** Tellurium	53 **I** Iodine	54 **Xe** Xenon
75 **Re** Rhenium	76 **Os** Osmium	77 **Ir** Iridium	78 **Pt** Platinum	79 **Au** Gold	80 **Hg** Mercury	81 **Tl** Thallium	82 **Pb** Lead	83 **Bi** Bismuth	84 **Po** Polonium	85 **At** Astatine	86 **Rn** Radon
107 **Bh** Bohrium	108 **Hs** Hassium	109 **Mt** Meit-nerium	110 **Ds** Darmstadt-ium	111 **Rg** Roent-genium							

The metals beneath this line are two groups of chemically similar elements. They are almost always set apart so that the table will fit across a page.

63 **Eu** Europium	64 **Gd** Gado-linium	65 **Tb** Terbium	66 **Dy** Dyspro-sium	67 **Ho** Holmium	68 **Er** Erbium	69 **Tm** Thulium	70 **Yb** Ytterbium
95 **Am** Amer-icium	96 **Cm** Curium	97 **Bk** Berkelium	98 **Cf** Califor-nium	99 **Es** Einstein-ium	100 **Fm** Fermium	101 **Md** Mende-levium	102 **No** Nobelium

KEY TO ELEMENT COLORS

- Alkali metals
- Alkaline earth metals
- Transition metals
- Lanthanides
- Actinides
- Metals in mixed groups
- Metalloids
- Nonmetals
- Noble gases

CREW

Eight rowers sit poised to move, four oars to one side and four to the other. They are still. The forces acting on them are balanced. Suddenly, with their oars just above the water, they bend their knees, slide forward, drop their oars into the water, and pull. The boat, called a *shell,* blasts into motion. This is the sport called *crew.* The force the rowers exert on the water—a force generated by their muscles and delivered by the oar—is greater than the force of the water pushing back against the oar. These unbalanced forces make the boat move. Before the shell slows down, the oars are already back in the water, pulling again. When the eight rowers pull together, they keep the boat steadily moving toward the finish line.

ALL TOGETHER NOW ▼

A boat floats because the force of the water pushing up on it balances the force of gravity pulling down on it. For a boat to move, some force—a propeller, a paddle, an oar—has to push it or pull it in a direction. Rowing with at least one other rower, each using one oar, is called *sweep rowing.* Each sweep of the oar through the water is called a *stroke.* Eight rowers can generate tremendous force—as long as everyone's stroke is perfectly synchronized.

An eight-person shell—called an *eight*—is about 58 feet (17.7 m) long. It is made of a lightweight carbon fiber, and weighs only about 200 pounds (90.7 kg).

The oar is held in place by an oarlock. The oarlock serves as a fulcrum, or balancing point, for the oar, which acts as a lever.

WHERE OAR AND WATER MEET ▶

The flat end of the oar is called the *blade*. Rowers turn the blade perpendicular to the water so it slices into the water easily and pushes the maximum amount of water out of the way. Most of the force of the stroke comes from the rowers' legs, which press against a fixed piece called a *footplate*. Rowers start in a coiled position, with their knees bent. Uncoiling provides the force.

If an oar blade gets stuck in the water—called "catching a crab"— the force on the handle can be strong enough to throw the rower out of the boat.

Shells are narrow and tippy. They are set up with oars on alternating sides for balance. Boats set up for rowers using two oars are called *sculls*.

CRITTERCAM

Greg Marshall, a marine biologist and filmmaker, got the idea for equipping animals with cameras in 1986, when he saw a suckerfish attached to a shark. If he could attach a camera to a shark, what great things would he see? Marshall began to develop a camera that could be attached to wild animals. Not all of his first attempts succeeded, but he persisted and developed a camera that worked. Now Crittercams are used as tools for research supported by National Geographic to help scientists study animals in their natural habitats. The Crittercam has helped scientists understand the habitat of the endangered Hawaiian monk seal. It has shown how tiger sharks interact with each other. It's shed light on what happens during a sea turtle's journey. Since 2002, the cameras have also been used to study the behavior of land animals, such as African lions and grizzly bears. These cameras can go where people cannot, and sneak peeks at animals' hidden lives.

did you know?
PENGUINS HELPED WIN AN OSCAR. CRITTERCAM WAS USED TO CAPTURE FOOTAGE FOR THE FILM *MARCH OF THE PENGUINS.*

A PENGUIN'S-EYE VIEW ▶

Here's a penguin's-eye view from a chinstrap penguin swimming near its companions on an iceberg in Antarctica. Scientists can study penguins as they catch fish during long underwater dives. Then they use the information in combination with other measurements, such as depth and location, to get a full picture of the penguin's habits.

A streamlined aluminum or titanium case protects the camera and equipment inside.

Hose clamps hold the Crittercam's casing in place.

A strong harness holds the camera to the penguin's back.

▲ HOLD ON TIGHT—OFF WE GO!

For this emperor penguin, a harness attachment for the camera works best. Suction cups work with smooth skinned creatures, such as whales. Fin clamps work on finned fish. Adhesives stick to monk seals, who spend much of their time on dry beaches. Each Crittercam is specially equipped: some with audio recording devices, some with headlights or attachments for night vision. Crittercams are released from the animal's body remotely. A computer inside marine Crittercams is programmed to release at a certain time, after which the Crittercam detaches from the animal and floats to the water's surface. Land Crittercams are released when scientists send a signal to release it.

CRYSTALS

Crystals form amazing shapes because their atoms and molecules are bonded together in an orderly, regular, repeated pattern. The pattern gives them their straight edges and smooth faces. But crystals aren't just flashy gems. Everyday things, such as sugar and salt, are also crystals. Scientists classify crystals in many different ways. One is based on the way their molecules or atoms are bonded. Some crystals are molecules that are weakly bonded together, such as ice, or rock candy made from sugar. Salt, an ionic crystal, has stronger bonds, because its atoms are bonded by the attraction of oppositely charged particles called *ions*. Salt dissolves in water, but if the water evaporates, crystals of salt form again. In metallic crystals, atoms are packed tightly to form a highly dense structure. Diamonds are called *covalent* crystals, because their atoms are bonded by sharing an electron. These bonds are extremely strong.

Axinite crystals are flattened and wedge-shaped.

did you know?

THE WORLD'S LARGEST CRYSTALS ARE ALMOST 40 FEET (ABOUT 12 M) LONG AND WEIGH ALMOST 60 TONS. THEY ARE GYPSUM CRYSTALS, LOCATED DEEP WITHIN THE CAVE OF CRYSTALS IN MEXICO.

PLEASE PASS THE SALT ▼

Southern France is famous for its seriously salty scenery. Located on the Mediterranean coast, the Camargue region is filled with inland salt lagoons that evaporate in the summer sun, leaving large piles of sea salt behind. The salt piles form huge mounds, some of which can grow up to 26 feet (about 8 m) tall. These salt mounds support a thriving salt industry in Camargue. Now, if only they had a pretzel factory nearby!

CRYSTAL SYSTEMS ▶

Crystals can be categorized by the arrangement of their atoms, called *lattices*. Imagine that a baseball represents an atom. If you arrange baseballs into a cube, you form what's called a *unit cell*. If you stack this cube onto another cube, you form a lattice. The shape of the unit cell is important. For example, both graphite and diamond consist only of carbon atoms. But because graphite and diamond have different shaped unit cells, they have different properties. Graphite is black and soft enough to lubricate plastic, metal, or wood, while diamond is clear and hard enough to cut many materials, including glass. The drawings on the right show various shapes of unit cells.

Cubic (or Isometric): halite (rock salt), diamond, pyrope (a type of garnet), spinel

Orthorhombic: aragonite, olivine, topaz, sulfur, tanzanite

Hexagonal/Trigonal (two similar systems): graphite, forms of beryl (aquamarine and emerald); forms of quartz (amethyst, ruby, sapphire)

Tetragonal: zircon, cassiterite (tin oxide), rutile (titanium oxide)

Triclinic: axinite, turquoise, rhodonite, wollastonite

Monoclinic: gymsum, malachite, talc, muscovite, azurite

Aquamarine crystals are used as gemstones.

Talc crystals break off in flakes that feel soapy.

Topaz crystals are shaped like prisms or double pyramids. They come in a variety of colors.

DATING ROCKS

A tree has rings, but how do you tell the age of a rock? Rocks have built-in clocks. Some elements in rocks go through a process called *radioactive decay.* The atoms of these elements emit particles from their nuclei. Over millions of years, this decay causes one type of atom to become another type. Take the element uranium, for example, a radioactive metal found in many rocks. Some forms of uranium decay into the element lead. If geologists count the atoms of lead in a rock sample, and compare it with the number of uranium atoms, they can tell how old the rock is. How? In the same way that we know how long it takes a log to burn, geologists know how long it takes uranium to decay into lead. So, the more lead in the rock, the older it is, because it has spent more time decaying.

did you know?
THE OLDEST KNOWN ROCK FORMATIONS ON EARTH CAN BE FOUND IN GREENLAND. THEY ARE THOUGHT TO BE 3.8 BILLION YEARS OLD.

DATING CAVE PAINTINGS ▼

Scientists can also date matter that was once living, such as bones and fabric. In the Pech Merle cave in France, the prehistoric artists used tiny amounts of charcoal in their black paint. Scientists measured the small amount of the radioactive form of carbon, carbon-14, that was in the charcoal to estimate that the paintings were created about 25,000 B.C. Scientists use different radioactive elements depending on what elements make up the item being dated. For instance, potassium-40 is used to date moon rocks, because they contain trace amounts of this radioactive element.

RESEARCH TOOLS ▲

Radioactive elements have what is called a *half-life:* the length of time it takes for half the atoms in element A to decay into element B. Using a tool called a *mass spectrometer,* a scientist finds that half of the atoms in a sample are A and half are B. If A has a half-life of 100 years, and half its atoms have decayed into B, the rock sample must be 100 years old. The elements used to date rocks have incredibly long half-lives. Uranium-238, for example, has a half-life of about 4.5 billion years!

Stromatolites are rocklike structures made of layers of primitive microorganisms, such as algae and bacteria, pressed together with layers of mineral deposits. Fossil stromatolites represent some of the first forms of life on Earth and have been found in rocks dated at 3.5 billion years old.

Some moon rocks collected by Apollo astronauts ranged from 3 to 4.6 billion years old.

A pair of fossilized tree cones dates from between 65 and 145 million years ago.

LAYERS UPON LAYERS ▲

Scientists often use more than one technique to date rocks. Rock layers provide a way of learning what's called the *relative age* of rocks and fossils. Older rocks are usually in the bottom layers, while younger rocks are on top. This helps scientists infer the relative age of fossils that are found in different layers of rock.

DEEP SEA VENTS

Deep sea vents are like rocky, underwater chimneys. In fact, they are often called *smokers,* because they spew plumes of hot, mineral-rich fluid that look like chimney smoke. They occur thousands of feet below the ocean surface, around the places where tectonic plates—huge pieces of Earth's crust—move away from one another. These places are called *mid-ocean ridges.* The vents form when cold water sinks into cracks around these ridges. Magma, molten rock deep within Earth, heats the water, which then rises back up through the ocean floor. Even though the sun's rays cannot reach deep sea vents, hundreds of organisms live around them. How? Instead of converting sunlight into energy through photosynthesis, these deep sea vent communities get energy through chemicals coming out of the vents, in a process called *chemosynthesis.* Could this be how organisms first developed on Earth?

WHAT'S FOR DINNER? ▼
The image below compares photosynthesis and chemosynthesis. The chemosynthetic cycle begins with bacteria. Bacteria feed on chemicals released by the vents. Smaller animals prey on these bacteria and then larger animals feed on the smaller ones.

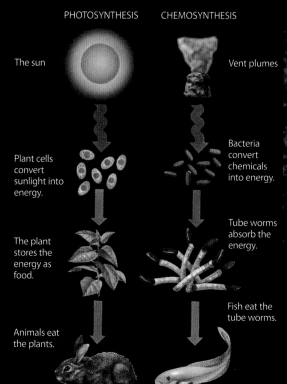

PHOTOSYNTHESIS   CHEMOSYNTHESIS

The sun   Vent plumes

Plant cells
convert
sunlight into
energy.

Bacteria
convert
chemicals
into energy.

The plant
stores the
energy as
food.

Tube worms
absorb the
energy.

Fish eat the
tube worms.

Animals eat
the plants.

TOTALLY TUBULAR WORMS ▶
Tube worms look like long
tubes of red lipstick. They are
huge animals—up to 8 feet (about
2.4 m) long, although most of
their bodies are usually hidden
in the tubes. They have a special
relationship with bacteria. The
bacteria live inside the worms,
turning chemicals from the vents
into nutrients for the worms. The
worms in turn may become food
for fish and crabs. Yum!

This is a black smoker.
Smokers can also be white,
clear, or gray, depending
on the minerals that are
dissolved in the fluid.

◀ MARINE LIFE AROUND A VENT
Deep sea vents form a unique ecosystem for the
creatures that live there. As a matter of fact, it is one of
the most extreme environments on Earth. The creatures
that live in vent communities have adapted to live
in total darkness. They endure freezing-cold water,
scorching-hot vents, and pressures great enough to
crush a human skull! More than 500 different organisms
have been discovered near deep sea vents. These
include strange and wonderful creatures such as giant
clams, furry "yeti" crabs, vent crabs, and soft-bellied
spaghetti worms. Scientists believe these creatures are
similar to early life forms on Earth.

 did you know? EVEN THOUGH VENTS CAN REACH TEMPERATURES OF 752°F
(400°C), HIGH PRESSURE KEEPS THE WATER FROM BOILING.
....

DEFIBRILLATORS

"Clear!" yells the doctor, as a jolt of electricity goes through a patient's heart. The machine the doctor is using is called a *defibrillator,* and many people are alive because of it. To understand how a defibrillator can save lives, you need to know how the heart works. The heart works by sending an electric signal across the muscle fibers that make it beat. It creates its own natural rhythm. When this rhythm is interrupted or becomes irregular, the heart cannot pump blood correctly and may even stop beating. A defibrillator resets the heart using a sudden shock of electricity. The powerful shock momentarily stops all functioning of the heart, including its own electric signals. This gives the heart a chance to restart with its own rhythm. Defibrillators can be external boxes, implanted units, and even wearable packs.

AUTOMATED EXTERNAL DEFIBRILLATOR (AED) ▼

The operator of an AED holds the two paddles on the patient's chest. Electrodes on the bottom of the paddles conduct electricity from the box to the patient's body. A microprocessor monitors the heart's rhythm. If the patient's beat becomes too erratic, the AED issues an alarm for the operator. The operator makes sure everyone is "clear" and away from the body before pressing the trigger and delivering an electric shock to the body.

Pressing the trigger shocks the patient and can sometimes result in muscle contractions which cause the body to jump slightly.

It takes the AED a few seconds to monitor the heart's rhythm and determine if a shock is needed.

MOBILE AED ▶

Some AEDs are portable and allow people who are at high risk for heart problems to carry one with them at all times. Like all AEDs, these units store a charge internally and then use the human body as the connector between electrodes. One electrode releases the high-energy shock, which then travels through the body to the other electrode. The body conducts the electricity in the same way a wire placed across a battery's terminals does.

did you know? ....

ONCE ELECTRODES ARE ATTACHED, MANY AED UNITS ARE CAPABLE OF EMITTING A SHOCK TO THE PATIENT'S HEART ON THEIR OWN, WITH NO FURTHER INPUT FROM AN OPERATOR. THIS HAS ALLOWED EVEN UNTRAINED PEOPLE TO SAVE LIVES.

▼ WHEN THE HEART'S SIGNAL GOES FLAT

The heart is an amazing organ that must work continuously throughout life with no breaks. Its signature beat is shown as an electronic signal shaped like the one below. When this beat is interrupted, a person can die very quickly. If the heart enters cardiac arrest, then it has stopped beating and its signal goes flat. A defibrillator must be used either before this happens or immediately afterward.

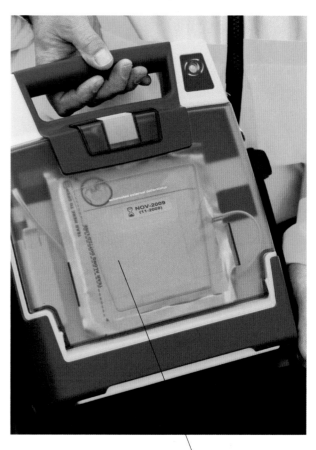

This pattern of small, larger, then small waves indicates a normal heartbeat.

This AED unit has adhesive electrodes that must be stuck on the patient's chest to monitor the heart's rhythm.

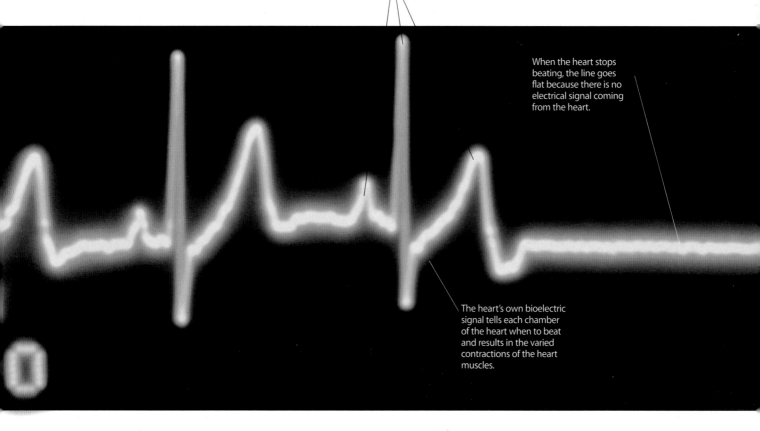

When the heart stops beating, the line goes flat because there is no electrical signal coming from the heart.

The heart's own bioelectric signal tells each chamber of the heart when to beat and results in the varied contractions of the heart muscles.

DIGESTION

You walk into the kitchen and smell something delicious. Your mouth starts watering. This fluid, called *saliva*, contains the first of many chemicals that help your body carry out the amazing process called *digestion*. When you eat food, your body takes the nutrients it needs, and gets rid of everything else. Digestion breaks down food into smaller molecules that can be absorbed into the bloodstream and distributed to cells throughout the body. The organs that help digest food, absorb nutrients, and get rid of waste are called the *digestive system*. The system includes the digestive tract, a series of hollow organs that connect to form a long, twisting, muscular tube. This tube consists of the mouth, esophagus, stomach, small intestine, large intestine, and rectum. The digestive system also relies on three other organs that help break down food—the liver, pancreas, and gall bladder.

▼ DOWN THE TUBE

The food travels down your throat into your esophagus. This muscular tube pushes the food into your stomach. Here, muscle contractions churn the food with hydrochloric acid and enzymes—substances that speed up chemical reactions. The enzymes help break down the food. Luckily, a layer of mucus protects your stomach lining from being digested by the acid. The food becomes a thick liquid, which the stomach slowly empties into the small intestine.

Stomach lining

Enzymes

Mucus

Hydrochloric acid

Gastric pits in the stomach wall secrete acid, enzymes, and mucus.

The pancreatic duct carries enzymes from the pancreas to the small intestine.

The bile duct carries bile from the gall bladder to the small intestine.

ALONG THE WAY ▶

After food leaves the stomach, it travels to the first segment of the small intestine, called the *duodenum*. Here, other substances are added to the liquid going into the small intestine—bile produced in the liver and stored in the gall bladder, plus enzymes produced in the pancreas. These substances help digest fats, proteins, and starches.

Duodenum

One of the salivary glands

A salivary duct

Tongue

Throat (pharynx)

Esophagus

Liver

Stomach

▼ BREAKING IT DOWN

Small only in diameter, the small intestine is
actually a twisty tube about 20 feet (about 6 m)
long. Its first job is to break down food, using
bile—a fluid produced by the liver—and pancreatic
enzymes. Next, the nutrient molecules are
absorbed through the small intestine's walls and
enter the bloodstream. Millions of tiny fingerlike
structures called *villi* line these walls. By increasing
the surface area, they allow more absorption.
Whatever hasn't been absorbed—water and
undigested food—moves into the large intestine.

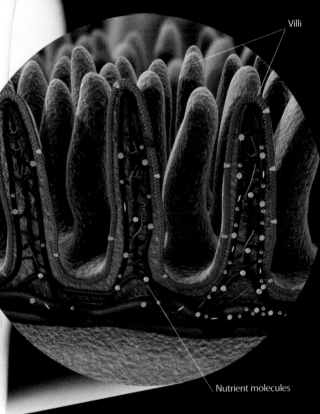

Villi

Nutrient molecules

◄ COMING TO AN END

The large intestine acts like a
giant sponge, absorbing water
into the bloodstream. Bacteria
digest any remaining food.
Everything else moves into a
short tube at the end of the
large intestine called the *rectum*.
Here, waste is compressed and
stored until the body gets rid of
it in a bowel movement.

Small intestine

Large intestine (colon)

Rectum

Appendix

DIGITAL CAMERA

Like all cameras, digital cameras start with the same source: light reflected from a landscape, a flower, or a smiling face. Cameras use lenses to focus, or gather, this light. The lens directs the light onto a light-sensitive site inside the camera. In a film camera, the light-sensitive site is the film, which changes chemically to record, or store, the image. In a digital camera, the light falls on a sensor made up of millions of light-sensitive squares. Each square on the sensor captures one square of the scene. That information is converted into an electrical signal. Software directs the process of putting the squares back together to make a picture, the way tiles come together to make a mosaic.

A removable memory card stores the images as digital files.

LENSES ▼

Light waves slow down when they hit a piece of glass or plastic, such as a lens. Lenses bend the light as it passes through. Cameras like the one shown here use lenses with different curves, which photographers switch depending on the type of picture they want to take. Telephoto lenses are inside long tubes, like the one shown below. They capture a small portion of the scene in front of them, and fill the picture area with that portion. A wide angle lens takes in a wider portion of the scene in front of it, and crams it all into the picture area.

IMAGE SENSOR

After the light passes through the lens, it hits the rectangular device called the *image sensor*, where the lens meets the body of the camera. The image sensor is actually a grid made up of millions of light-sensitive squares, or cells, called *pixels*. The word *pixel* refers both to each cell on the sensor, and to each tiny square of information the cell detects. The sensor communicates what it senses by sending an electric signal.

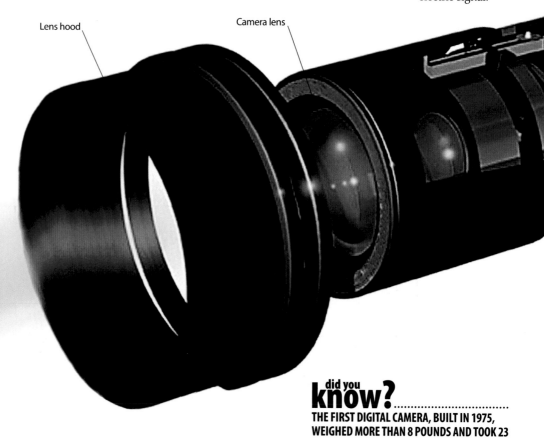

Lens hood

Camera lens

did you know?...............

THE FIRST DIGITAL CAMERA, BUILT IN 1975, WEIGHED MORE THAN 8 POUNDS AND TOOK 23 SECONDS TO RECORD A PICTURE.

VIEWING SCREEN ▼

The viewing screen works as a computer's screen does. An electrical signal from the sensor lights up thousands of tiny red, green, and blue cells. These colors of light mix to make a multicolored map of pixels that shows up as an image on the viewing screen.

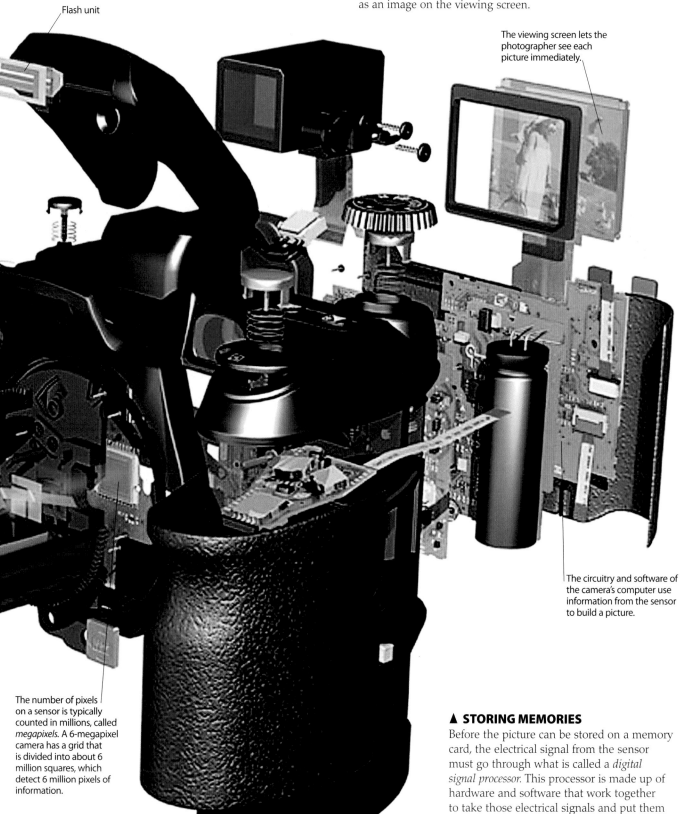

Flash unit

The viewing screen lets the photographer see each picture immediately.

The circuitry and software of the camera's computer use information from the sensor to build a picture.

The number of pixels on a sensor is typically counted in millions, called *megapixels*. A 6-megapixel camera has a grid that is divided into about 6 million squares, which detect 6 million pixels of information.

Battery

▲ STORING MEMORIES

Before the picture can be stored on a memory card, the electrical signal from the sensor must go through what is called a *digital signal processor*. This processor is made up of hardware and software that work together to take those electrical signals and put them back together again to form the picture. A lot of digital information can be stored in a very small space.

Who says that dinosaurs are ancient history? Even now, scientists are discovering new things about these Mesozoic beasts! In 1995, a fossil hunter in Argentina discovered the skeleton of a new species of dinosaur. Scientists measured its bones and found that this giant meat-eating creature was bigger than *T. rex!* Maybe that's why they named it *Giganotosaurus.* Along with new discoveries, there are also new arguments brewing among scientists. Paleontologists, the scientists who study dinosaurs, are arguing about whether dinosaurs were endotherms, controlling their own body temperature, or ectotherms, whose temperature changed with their environment. Recent discoveries show that some dinosaurs were quick and active, and not slow, lumbering reptiles. Now, many scientists are also saying that dinosaurs are not extinct. Most paleontologists believe that modern birds, such as ostriches, are related to some of the dinosaurs that lived 100 to 200 million years ago.

fleshy nasal passages. These helped the animals gain or lose heat when they breathed air.

These sharp, sawlike teeth were perfect for tearing meat.

Large inner ears suggest sensitive hearing.

Large eyes suggest well-developed vision.

did you know? PLANT-EATING DINOSAURS COULD GROW OVER 100 FEET (30 M) LONG AND WEIGH AS MUCH AS 33 CARS! ....

◄ TROODON

The *Troodon,* whose name means "wounding tooth," was one of the first dinosaurs discovered in North America. Studying the *Troodon's* skeleton has given scientists plenty of clues about what it was like. They believe it was a small, quick predator with keen vision and hearing. Because of the large size of its braincase, scientists think the *Troodon* was one of the smartest dinosaurs around.

Big, flexible hands were used for grasping.

Some pterosaurs had flaps on their tails to keep them stable during flight.

PTEROSAUR ►

It's not hard to figure out why the pterosaur's name means "wing lizard." However, it may be surprising to know that these flying creatures were not dinosaurs, even though they lived during the same time. Dinosaurs were land animals who never flew until some of their descendants developed feathers and were able to fly. Pterosaurs flew using wings with no feathers. They were relatives of the dinosaurs who ranged in size from tiny birds to airplanes. Their bones were hollow, though, so these lightweight winged lizards could soar easily through the skies.

Long, thin legs helped the *Troodon* move quickly.

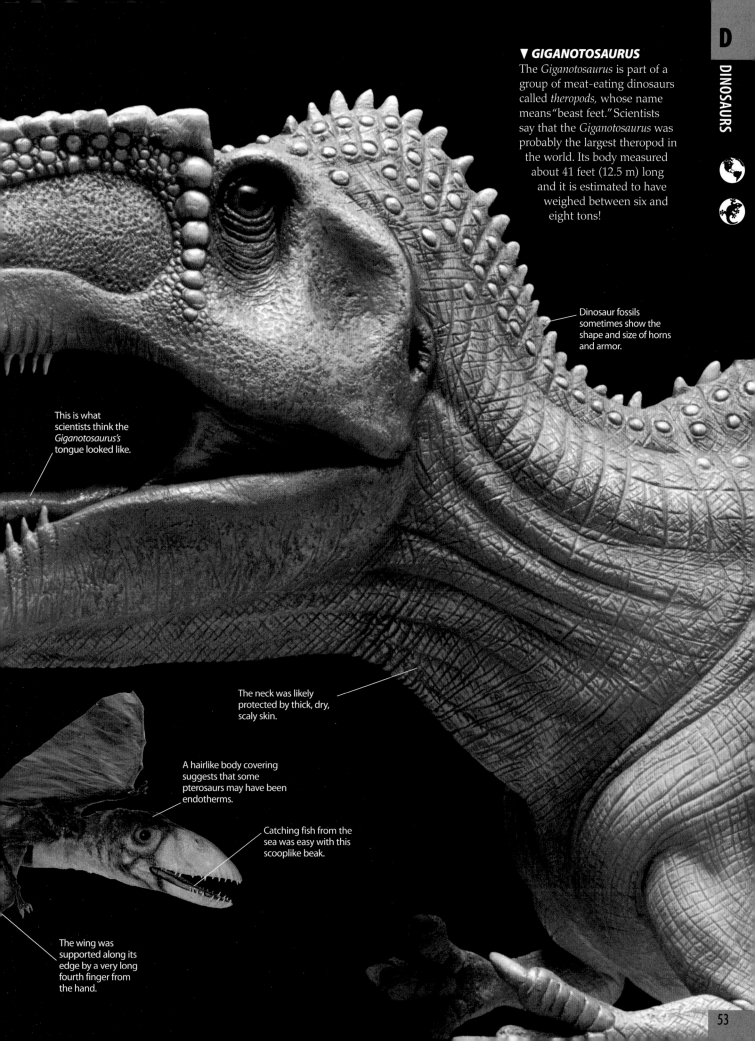

▼ *GIGANOTOSAURUS*

The *Giganotosaurus* is part of a group of meat-eating dinosaurs called *theropods,* whose name means "beast feet." Scientists say that the *Giganotosaurus* was probably the largest theropod in the world. Its body measured about 41 feet (12.5 m) long and it is estimated to have weighed between six and eight tons!

Dinosaur fossils sometimes show the shape and size of horns and armor.

This is what scientists think the *Giganotosaurus's* tongue looked like.

The neck was likely protected by thick, dry, scaly skin.

A hairlike body covering suggests that some pterosaurs may have been endotherms.

Catching fish from the sea was easy with this scooplike beak.

The wing was supported along its edge by a very long fourth finger from the hand.

DNA CONNECTIONS

Did you realize that a fish is related to a banana tree? In fact, all living things on Earth—people, zebras, yeast, and plants—are related and share a fundamental structure of life: DNA. DNA, short for deoxyribonucleic acid, is a large molecule that carries the information an organism needs to grow and develop. Simple one-celled organisms have DNA, and multicelled organisms, such as animals, plants, and fungi, have DNA. By comparing the DNA of two different species, scientists can estimate how closely they are related. In general, closely related species have more DNA in common than distantly related species. Organisms of the same species hardly differ in their DNA at all. For example, your DNA is 99.9 percent identical to the person next to you and to all humans on Earth.

DNA COUSINS ▶
Scientists can sometimes use DNA to estimate how closely related different species are. Scientists can compare the DNA sequence—the arrangement of the DNA components—of two species. In general, the more differences there are between the sequences, the more time has passed since these two species shared a common ancestor. For instance, chimpanzees and orangutans share about 97 percent of their DNA sequence. This means that they are very closely related.

Ninety percent of DNA sequences that cause disease in humans are the same in mice, explaining their popularity in disease research.

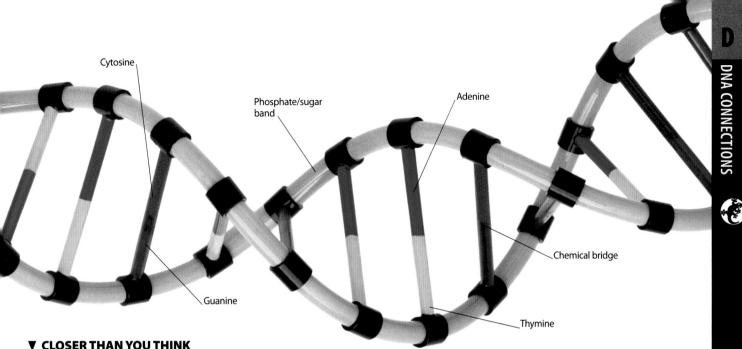

Cytosine

Phosphate/sugar band

Adenine

Chemical bridge

Guanine

Thymine

▼ CLOSER THAN YOU THINK

This orangutan and his apple look as if they have nothing in common. The apple is a plant, while the orangutan is an animal. The apple has a waxy covering, and the orangutan has skin covered in fur. But despite the differences in appearance, both the apple and the orangutan were built from instructions coded in DNA. Their DNA, and the DNA of every other living thing, is composed of the same four chemicals: A, G, C, and T.

Those four chemicals are all that is needed to produce living things as different as an apple and an orangutan, bacteria and mushrooms, an oak tree and a bumblebee.

▲ STRUCTURE OF DNA

The shape of a DNA strand is like a spiraling ladder. Look at the model above. Along the sides, you can see the chain of sugar and phosphate molecules that make up the backbone of the ladder. The rungs of the ladder are formed by chemicals called *bases*. The four bases found in DNA are adenine (A), guanine (G), cytosine (C), and thymine (T). A single base sticks out from the backbone and forms a chemical bond with the base directly across from it. These two bonded bases are called *a base pair*. Adenine always pairs with thymine, and cytosine always pairs with guanine.

BLUE ZEBRA CICHLID ▲

Over time, small changes to DNA, called *mutations,* can occur. The more time that passes, the more mutations can happen. These mutations can result in new species forming. This blue zebra cichlid is one of 2,000 species of cichlids that has evolved in the last 10,000 years. That amounts to about one new species every five years—one of the fastest evolutionary waves on record.

did you know?..........................

HUMANS CARRY THE DNA SEQUENCE FOR A TAIL! BUT DURING EARLY DEVELOPMENT, ANOTHER SEQUENCE OVERRIDES IT.

DNA EVIDENCE

How can scientists use genetic information to identify a criminal suspect? The answer lies in our DNA. Every person's DNA—short for deoxyribonucleic acid—is 99.9 percent the same. It is the 0.1 percent difference that can help solve crimes. Crime investigators look at 13 regions of human DNA. These areas have a great deal of variation. When DNA from a crime scene and DNA from a suspect match all 13 regions, the probability that they are from the same person is almost 100 percent. It takes only one difference in one region to prove they are not from the same person. People imprisoned before DNA evidence was available have been proven innocent and released because of that difference.

WHOSE BLOOD? ►
An individual's DNA is the same in every cell, including blood cells. If scientists collect the DNA from blood at a crime scene, they can use the particular arrangement of molecules, called *DNA sequences*, to identify a criminal or a victim. Even if no one saw the crime, the DNA might be able to tell police who was involved.

Human skin   Human hair

Loose scales of skin around the follicle

HAIR FOLLICLE ▲
DNA is found in the sac, called a *hair follicle*, where a hair attaches to the body, as well as in skin, bone, teeth, saliva, sweat, earwax, and even dandruff!

▲ EVEN HAIR HAS DNA
Criminal cases have been solved by DNA analysis of saliva on cigarettes, stamps, cups, or mouth openings on ski masks used in a crime. Even a single hair, without the follicle, can reveal information. The DNA in hair, bones, and teeth comes from a cell's mitochondria rather than from its nucleus. The DNA that is in the mitochondria, unlike the DNA that is in the nucleus, does not contain all of the information, because it is inherited only from the mother. However, it lasts longer, so it is often used in older unsolved "cold" cases. It can be used to exclude a suspect, but not to convict one.

Heat, moisture, sunlight, bacteria, and mold can affect DNA enough to make it unusable.

These bands show the distinctive pattern of an individual's DNA.

DNA PROFILING

DNA identification is based on probabilities. The probability that DNA from two individuals matches in one region is about 1 in 10 (1/10). The probability of a match in two regions is 1/10 x 1/10, or 1 in 100 (1/100), and so on. So, for example, the probability that your DNA matches someone else's in all 13 regions is 1 in ten trillion (1/10,000,000,000,000).

U.S. laboratories test hundreds of thousands of DNA sequences each year. Here is a magnified view of a DNA sequence.

did you know? SCIENTISTS USUALLY NEED ONLY A FEW CELLS TO COMPLETE A DNA PROFILE.

DOLPHINS

"Hoop, ball, fetch." Would you be able to understand this command in American Sign Language? Bottlenose dolphins that were involved in language research in Hawaii could understand the command in a similar form of sign language. It means "bring the ball to the hoop." These dolphins could also tell whether an object was in their tank or not. When given the sign for "basket," a dolphin would swim around looking for a basket. Then it would push either a "yes" or "no" paddle to say whether a basket was there. Self-awareness and the abilities to communicate and use tools are all considered signs of intelligence. Like primates, dolphins are capable of all of these skills and of learning. "How is this possible?" scientists wonder. The dolphin brain is different from the primate brain in the way that it's organized and how it functions. Scientists are studying these differences to help solve the mystery of dolphin intelligence.

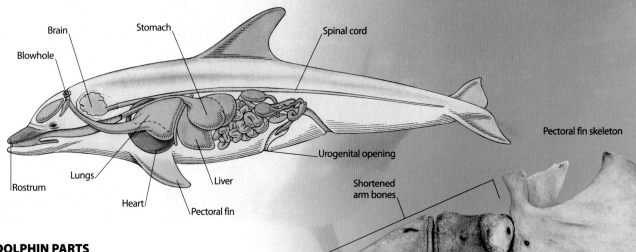

Brain   Stomach   Spinal cord

Blowhole

Urogenital opening

Pectoral fin skeleton

Rostrum

Lungs   Liver   Shortened arm bones

Heart   Pectoral fin   Scapula, or shoulder blade

Finger bones

DOLPHIN PARTS

A dolphin's anatomy is similar to our own. Although dolphins don't have hands, some have learned to use tools. Some dolphins in Australia use sea sponges for hunting. They place a sponge on their rostrums, or snouts, when they forage for food. The sponges protect the dolphins from injury. Researchers believe mother dolphins teach this trick to their daughters—evidence that dolphins invent and pass on certain behaviors to their young.

These massive tails move in an up-and-down motion to propel dolphins through the water.

DOLPHIN COMMUNICATION

Bottlenose dolphins are very social creatures. They communicate by producing clicks and whistles. Researchers think that each dolphin develops its own signature whistle—like a name—in its first year of life. Dolphins not only produce their own signature whistle, they also learn the whistles of other dolphins. Lost dolphins can be heard producing frantic signature whistles. Some scientists think they are calling their friends.

 ONE RECENT STUDY SHOWED THAT DOLPHINS CAN RECOGNIZE THEMSELVES IN A MIRROR AND CAN NOTICE CHANGES IN THEIR APPEARANCE.

DOPPLER RADAR

If a thunderstorm, tornado, or hurricane is headed your way, you'd like to know about it before it gets to you. One of the tools meteorologists use to predict the path of a storm is Doppler radar. Doppler radar uses radio waves to determine the direction, speed, and strength of a storm. The National Weather Service manages a network of 159 NEXRAD—Next-Generation Radar—towers. Each tower looks like a giant soccer ball sitting on top of a pedestal. The towers send radio waves out in all directions. The radio waves reflect off small particles of dust, rain, or ice in the atmosphere. The towers can detect the reflected radio waves within a range of about 288 miles (463 km). Computers analyze the reflected radio waves to build up a picture of what is happening on the ground and in the sky.

The ball, called a *radome*, is made of weather-resistant material that prevents damage from ice buildup, wind, and rain.

INSIDE THE BALL ▲
The ball at the top of the NEXRAD tower protects an antenna inside it. The antenna sends and receives radio waves. Computers determine how far away a storm is by timing how long it takes for the radio waves to return to the antenna. The computers also determine the speed and direction of the storm by detecting tiny changes in the number of returning waves in a period of time—called *frequency*. A lower frequency means the storm is moving away from the antenna. A higher frequency means the storm is moving toward the antenna.

◄ **THUNDERSTORMS APPROACH**

This computer-generated weather map is a product of Doppler radar. It shows the path of a weather system and its precipitation. The map is updated every 6 minutes. Based on the radar's measurements, each color on the map represents an estimate of the amount of precipitation that will fall in 1 hour if the rate of precipitation does not change. The scale on the right shows the precipitation amounts for each color.

Light blue areas on the map indicate smaller amounts of detectable precipitation.

A white dot inside the darker red indicates the most intense rainfall.

U.S. east coast

did you
know?..............................
DOPPLER RADAR SPENDS ROUGHLY 7 SECONDS OF EACH HOUR SENDING OUT RADIO WAVES. IT SPENDS THE REST OF THE TIME DETECTING THE RETURNING WAVES.

DRAG RACING

Fire up your engine and get ready to fly! When the light turns green, the top fuel dragster—the fastest class of dragster—starts to move—*really* move! In 0.8 seconds, the dragster has already reached a speed of about 100 miles per hour (almost 161 km/h). By 4 seconds, it reaches its maximum speed of 300 miles per hour (almost 483 km/h). To reach such a high speed in a short period of time, the dragster must initially accelerate at close to 6 times the acceleration due to gravity. A military fighter jet accelerates this much when it is catapulted off the deck of an aircraft carrier. A space shuttle does not accelerate this much to break free of Earth's gravitational pull and enter space. One reason the dragster can accelerate so fast is its engine. The engine on a dragster delivers about 5,222 kilowatts of power. This is the equivalent of about 37 average automobile engines.

DECELERATION ▼

After its amazing acceleration, the car has to stop at the end of the track. A combination of brakes and parachutes gives the car a negative acceleration, or deceleration, that is as much as five times the acceleration due to gravity. A harness system and seat belt keep the driver from smashing through the windshield.

Cars traveling more than 150 miles per hour (241 km/h) are required to use a parachute to stop. Above 200 miles per hour (322 km/h), two parachutes are needed.

The fat rear tires produce a lot of friction against the track to help accelerate the car forward. They wear out after about 2 miles of use.

During deceleration, friction on the brakes heats them to a glowing red and sends up a cloud of smoke.

Weight transfers to the back of the car during acceleration and to the front of the car during deceleration. The wings here and in back of the car help control the car's contact with the track during this transfer.

◄ TOP FUEL DRAGSTER

During a single race, the dragster's powerful engine burns more than 4 gallons (15 L) of fuel. For the absolute best acceleration, top fuel cars burn nitromethane. The chemical bonds of nitromethane store more energy than those of gasoline. This allows the dragster to get more power from the engine.

The human body can take a high level of acceleration for only a short period of time. A typical ride lasts only about 4 seconds.

During the first 200 feet (about 61 m) of the run, the front tires don't touch the ground.

DRINKING WATER

Thirsty? There are more than 300 million trillion gallons of water (1,136 million trillion L) on Earth, but most of it will never reach your drinking glass. About 97 percent of the world's H_2O is salt water, and about another 2 percent is frozen in ice caps and glaciers. That leaves only about 1 percent of all Earth's water that is unfrozen and suitable for sipping. Less than 1 percent of that drinkable water is on the surface, in lakes and rivers. The rest of this precious resource is underground. Ancient civilizations found ways to tap into this water. Many people still use these methods today. No matter where you live, you need water. Why is water so essential? The human body cannot use oxygen, unlock nutrients from food, or prevent overheating without water. A few days without any water can lead to death.

ANCIENT ENGINEERING ▼

Most of the water we use comes from lakes and rivers, even though most of Earth's drinkable water lies in what are called *aquifers*—layers of earth saturated with water. In the arid Middle East, ancient engineers figured out how to use this groundwater by building water systems called *qanats*. These sophisticated systems, still used today, channel the water from an aquifer downhill, bringing it to the surface many miles away.

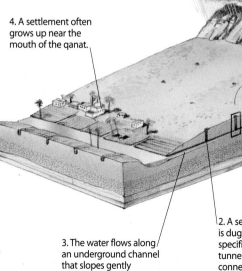

1. Rainwater runs down from the mountains and seeps into the ground.

4. A settlement often grows up near the mouth of the qanat.

Wells are used for ventilation while digging the tunnel, to repair the well shafts and channel when needed, and also to draw water.

Underground stream

2. A series of wells is dug, each to a specific depth. A tunnel is excavated, connecting the wells to form a channel.

3. The water flows along an underground channel that slopes gently downwards.

▲ WELL WATER

In some parts of the world, families carry all their water from the nearest well. A well provides access to groundwater, which is more plentiful and generally cleaner than surface water. Wells that are dug or bored into soft sediments are shallow, and often dry up or become contaminated. Much deeper wells, less prone to running dry, are made by drilling into rock layers.

LifeStraw

did you know?.............
DIVIDE YOUR WEIGHT (IN POUNDS) BY 2, AND YOU GET THE APPROXIMATE NUMBER OF OUNCES OF WATER YOU SHOULD DRINK EACH DAY. FOR A 130-POUND PERSON, THAT'S 65 OUNCES, OR ABOUT 2 QUARTS (2 L).

◀ DRINK IN GOOD HEALTH

Clean water is taken for granted in developed nations. In a typical day, the United States uses about 350 billion gallons of it. But one in three people around the world does not have adequate water. Many people in poorer nations are forced to drink contaminated water, leading to illness or death. This woman is drinking through a LifeStraw®, which cleans water by filtering out bacteria and viruses as the drinker sucks up water.

DUNES

In a village in the West African nation of Mauritania, homes are in danger. Houses in this arid desert are being swallowed by advancing sand dunes. A dune is a landform in motion, constantly shifting position as wind erosion moves particles of sand from one location and deposits them in another. Dunes form when wind carries sand-size particles in a jumping or bouncing motion, a process called *saltation*. As the wind carries the sand, the wind slows down. The wind then deposits the sand, often forming ripples that correspond to the lengths of the jumps. The wind continues to pick up and deposit sand in this way. Larger particles can creep along in the desert when they are hit by these saltating particles.

▼ DUNE DIRECTION

Which way are these dunes moving? A dune's shape tells its story. Dunes move toward their leeward side—the side opposite from the wind direction. Generally, the windward slope is less steep than the leeward slope. Surface ripples are also revealing. Those on the windward side are longer and shallower, while the ripples on the leeward sides are shorter and steeper. In this photo, the steeper slopes are to the right, so the dunes are moving in that direction.

Wind pushes sand up the windward slope. To move sand, wind must be fast enough to overcome surface friction.

Wind deposits sand down the leeward side, called the *slip face*. Its steepness is determined by the size and shape of sand grains.

WIND POWER ▶

Depending on its direction, wind sculpts dunes into different shapes. Barriers, such as rocks, affect dune shape dramatically. Wind blowing constantly from one direction forms classic curves, whereas wind blowing sometimes from one direction and sometimes from another creates a series of long, linear dunes. Star dunes are formed where wind blows from many directions.

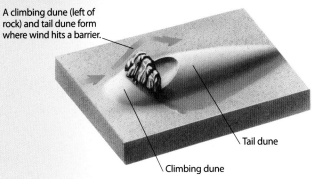

A climbing dune (left of rock) and tail dune form where wind hits a barrier.

Tail dune

Climbing dune

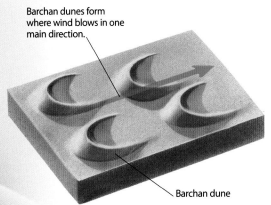

Barchan dunes form where wind blows in one main direction.

Barchan dune

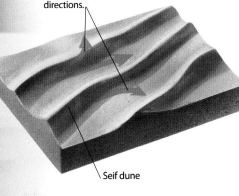

Seif dunes form where wind blows in two directions.

Seif dune

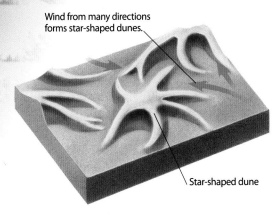

Wind from many directions forms star-shaped dunes.

Star-shaped dune

did you know?

SCIENTISTS ARE RESEARCHING WHY CERTAIN VERY DRY SAND DUNES IN CALIFORNIA, NEVADA, AND HAWAII EMIT SQUEAKING, BOOMING, OR SINGING SOUNDS WHEN THEY ARE DISTURBED.

DUST STORMS

Imagine you are outside on a sunny, blue-skied day. Suddenly, you look up and see a brown cloud on the horizon. An hour later, a howling wind is smothering you in a towering wall of dirt. You have just been caught in a dust storm! Dust storms are natural events in which soil particles are picked up and transported by the wind. They occur when large air masses near the ground are heated by the sun and rise quickly into the atmosphere. The rising warm air forces the cold air downward, creating winds strong enough to pick up loose dust and sand as they move across the land. Dust storms can be miles long, with walls of dust several thousand feet high. They can last from a few hours to a few days. Dust storms generally occur in dry, desert regions. They were common in the Great Plains region of the United States in the 1930s partly because the intensive cultivation of wheat in that region left the soil unprotected, and partly because of droughts and strong winds. This period of severe dust storms is known as the Dust Bowl.

SANDSTORMS ▶
This windy wall is a sandstorm blowing through the Kalahari Desert in southern Africa. Although they look similar, sandstorms are different from dust storms. The term sand refers to a soil particle that is 0.6 to 1 mm in size. Dust refers to a soil particle less than 0.6 mm in size. Sandstorms, then, are generally more powerful than dust storms because they have to carry larger particles.

did you know?
DUST FROM STORMS IN THE SAHARA DESERT IS A KEY SOURCE OF NUTRIENTS FOR PHYTOPLANKTON IN THE MEDITERRANEAN SEA.

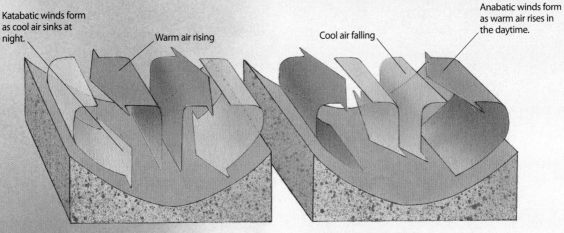

Katabatic winds form as cool air sinks at night.

Warm air rising

Cool air falling

Anabatic winds form as warm air rises in the daytime.

DOWNHILL WINDS ▲

Wind conditions can be very local, especially in areas with mountains and valleys. When mountain slopes grow cold at night, the air near the slopes becomes colder than the air in the valley. As this cool, dense air sinks down the slope to the valley floor, the warm air rises, creating a downhill wind, called *katabatic* wind, which can sometimes cause dust storms.

UPHILL WINDS ▲

During the day, the sun warms the mountain slopes. These slopes heat the nearby air. This warmed air expands upward. Air from the valley floor rises to replace the warmed air, resulting in an uphill wind called an *anabatic* wind.

Desert winds transport huge amounts of sediment that can be deposited more than 3,000 miles (about 5,000 km) from the source.

These African oryx have adapted to frequent sand and dust storms in the Kalahari Desert.

EARTH

It's the only home you know, but is it the only home out there? Earth has many things in common with the other planets in our solar system. It is a sphere. It follows an oval path around the sun. It rotates on an axis, which causes day and night. However, in one important way, Earth is unique. It is the only planet that we know of that is home to living things. No other planet has the conditions needed for life. Earth is near enough to the sun to keep living things warm, but not so near that living things are cooked by its heat. Earth is the only planet whose surface has lots of liquid water, which is necessary for all life as we know it. Surrounding Earth is a blanket of gases called the *atmosphere*. Nitrogen, oxygen, and carbon dioxide are the atmospheric gases that provide living things with the tools they need to harvest energy from sunlight and other materials on Earth's surface.

THE WATERY PLANET ▶

Water exists in three forms, or states, on Earth and in the atmosphere: solid, liquid, and gas. You can see evidence of all three in this picture. The blue oceans are water in its liquid state. The mountains are covered with water in its solid state—ice—making mountaintops snowy-white. When water becomes a gas—water vapor—it returns to the atmosphere, forming clouds.

Clouds of tiny water droplets swirl as if they were wisps of cotton in the atmosphere. When clouds build up and become saturated, the drops fall to Earth as rain.

THE SOLAR SYSTEM ▼

Eight planets orbit the sun. Mercury, Venus, Earth, and Mars are rocky, and Jupiter, Saturn, Uranus, and Neptune are giant balls of gas. Moons, dwarf planets, asteroids, meteoroids, and comets also inhabit the solar system. Moons are balls of rock that orbit planets, while asteroids are chunks of rock that orbit the sun. Comets are chunks of dust and ice that orbit the sun. Meteoroids are pieces that break off from asteroids and comets.

Scientists call Pluto a dwarf planet. Its orbit is at an angle to the orbits of Earth and the other planets.

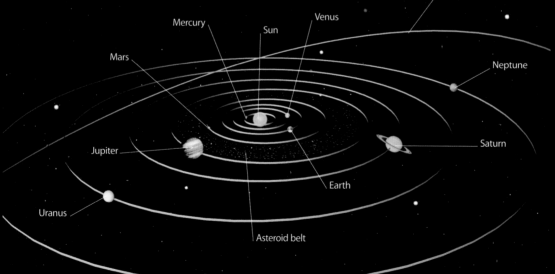

Mercury
Sun
Venus
Mars
Neptune
Jupiter
Saturn
Earth
Uranus
Asteroid belt

did you know?

GEOSCIENTISTS CALCULATE THAT THE TEMPERATURE AT THE CENTER OF EARTH'S CORE IS BETWEEN 8,000°F AND 10,000°F (ABOUT 4,427°C–5,538°C)!

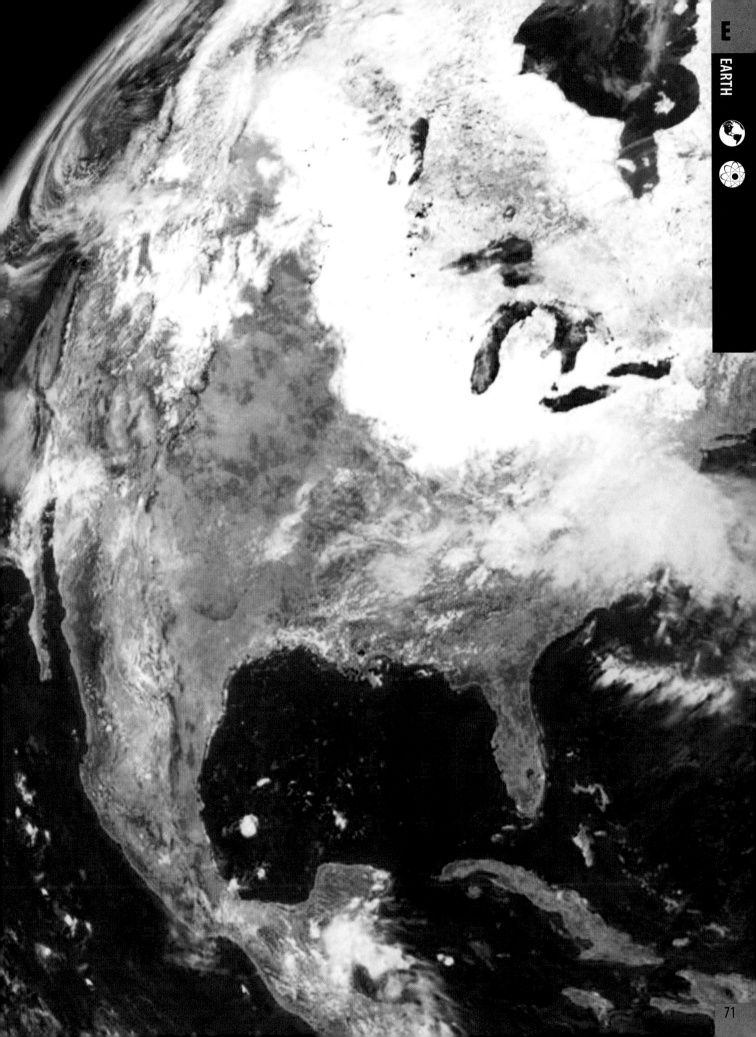

EARTHQUAKES

What causes Earth to shake? Earth's crust is made of about twelve blocks of rock, called *tectonic plates*, sitting on a layer of hot molten rock. Most earthquakes occur where two plates meet. Pressure builds up as the plates try to slide under, over, or past each other. At some point, the plates move into a position that results in an earthquake. Some quakes are so mild that they can't be felt, and others shake the ground violently, destroying roads and buildings. The vibrations, called *seismic waves*, travel both on and below Earth's surface. The type of area they travel through influences how much destruction the waves cause.

Cracks can form in the ground when tectonic plates move.

The epicenter is on the surface directly above the focus.

Seismic waves move out from the focus in circles. They can cause damage for great distances.

Seismic waves measured farther from the focus appear as shorter lines on a seismograph.

The focus is the point underground where an earthquake originates.

did you **know?**............
THE WORLD'S LARGEST RECORDED EARTHQUAKE TOOK PLACE IN CHILE IN 1960. IT WAS A 9.5 ON THE RICHTER SCALE.

HOW BIG WAS THAT QUAKE? ▲

The Richter scale records the magnitude of seismic waves. People usually don't feel earthquakes of 2.0 or less. Each whole-number increase indicates a tenfold increase in magnitude. A 5.0 is moderate, while a 6.0 is 10 times larger. Great earthquakes, of 8.0 or above, occur somewhere on Earth about once a year. Another scale, called the *Mercalli scale,* uses Roman numerals to rank earthquakes by how much damage they cause.

SEISMOGRAPHS MEASURE GROUND MOVEMENT ▶

An instrument called a *seismograph* records the seismic waves sent out by earthquakes. A pen makes a zigzag line when the ground under it moves. The bigger the movement sensed, the taller the line.

KOBE EARTHQUAKE ▼

In 1995, an earthquake of magnitude 7.2 on the Richter scale struck Kobe, Japan. The strong ground motions caused this expressway to collapse. Hundreds of thousands of buildings and homes were destroyed, and thousands of people were killed. The quake was a shindo 7 on a Japanese intensity scale that measures the degree of destruction from 0 to 7. Kobe was rebuilt with earthquake-resistant buildings and roads.

EARTH'S CORE

Science fiction stories tell of journeys to Earth's core, but you really don't
want to go there. We live on top of a thin, cool crust. Beneath it are
layers that get hotter and hotter the closer you get to the center of Earth.
To get to the center, you would have to travel about 3,958 miles (about
6,370 km). It's not too far, really—about the flying distance between
Miami, Florida, and Anchorage, Alaska. There in the center, you would
find a solid ball of iron and nickel—the inner core. The temperature
would be close to 10,000°F (about 5,500°C). Surrounding the inner
core is a layer of molten metals—the outer core. Here hot liquid metals
rise, cool off, and sink, creating convection currents. Heat from the core
causes similar currents in the layer between the core and the crust, called
the *mantle*. It is rock, but under such intense pressure and heat, the rock
can flow like a slow-moving liquid.

▼ EARTH'S SPACE SHIELD

Geophysicists believe that the currents within Earth's outer core
control Earth's magnetic field, called the *magnetosphere*. The
magnetosphere protects Earth by deflecting particles. A constant
stream of charged particles blows outward from the sun at more
than 1 million miles per hour. This solar wind would be deadly if we
did not have the protection of a giant magnetic field.

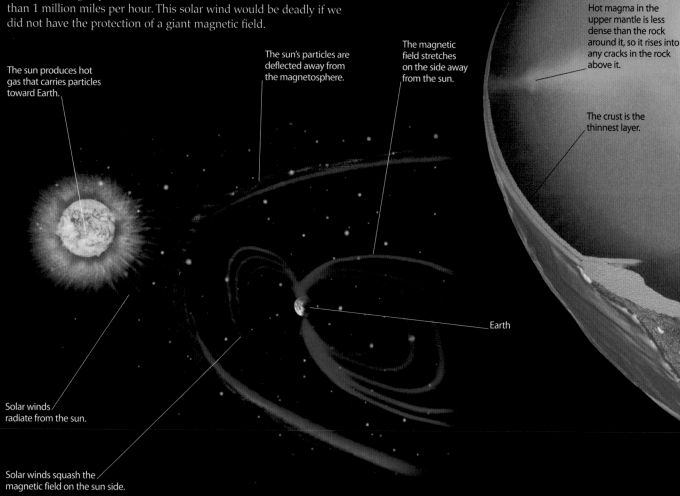

The sun produces hot gas that carries particles toward Earth.

The sun's particles are deflected away from the magnetosphere.

The magnetic field stretches on the side away from the sun.

Hot magma in the upper mantle is less dense than the rock around it, so it rises into any cracks in the rock above it.

The crust is the thinnest layer.

Earth

Solar winds radiate from the sun.

Solar winds squash the magnetic field on the sun side.

<h1>did you know?</h1>

EARTH'S INNER CORE ROTATES FASTER THAN THE REST OF THE PLANET. ABOUT EVERY 120 YEARS, THE CORE GAINS AN EXTRA DAY COMPARED WITH THE SURFACE.

The inner core is as hot as the sun's surface.

Swirling currents in the molten metal of the outer core generate Earth's magnetic field.

The rocky lower mantle is heated to 6,332°F (3,500°C) at its base. Heat rising from the core keeps the hot rock moving slowly.

◀ BIG MAGNET

We know that Earth is magnetic because compasses point to the place on Earth known as Earth's *magnetic north pole*. Radiating out from this imaginary line through the center of Earth are lines of magnetic force. Scientists think that the movement of molten metals taking place in Earth's core creates a circulating electric current that maintains Earth's magnetism.

ECHOLOCATION

Most animals use vision to find prey and travel through their world. But some animals use their ears to "see." These animals emit sounds (often clicks or squeaks) that travel in waves through air or water. When a sound wave encounters a solid object, it bounces back. By listening to this echo, animals can locate prey or obstacles. The echoes give information about an object's size, shape, distance, traveling speed, and direction of movement! This process is called *echolocation*. Some bats, birds, shrews, and marine animals use echolocation. The time it takes for an echo to return shows how far away prey is. The loudness of an echo can indicate the prey's size, distance, and even texture. Dolphins can detect prey from hundreds of yards or meters away, and bats can tell whether or not a moth is fuzzy. When bats begin a hunt, they may send out one sound per second. As they get close to their prey, however, they may emit 200 or more sounds per second.

▼ THE ECHO OF A WORM

Pygmy shrews weigh less than a penny and can fit on your thumbnail. They must eat every 15 to 30 minutes, 24 hours a day. When hunting prey, pygmy shrews make a rapid yawning motion. They aren't sleepy. They are emitting ultrasonic pulses of sound to echolocate prey, such as this worm. Pygmy shrews also use echolocation to find their way through piles of leaves or to navigate in underground tunnels.

Shrews have tiny eyes and must rely on touch (whiskers) and sound (echolocation) to locate prey.

Shrews have two sets of whiskers, which they can twitch 20 times per second to touch and determine characteristics of prey.

Shrews and moles eat insects and earthworms. Earthworms avoid sunlight, and instead come to the surface to feed at night.

DINING LATE ►

Bats have good eyesight, but they are nocturnal mammals. Many bats use echolocation to navigate and find food in the dark. Different types of bats use different echolocation frequencies. Scientists can record the sounds to identify bat types. Moths have evolved strategies to defend themselves from echolocating bats. Some have fuzzy wings that muffle the echo. Foul-tasting tiger moths send clicking noises out to bats, and bats avoid them.

did you
know?...........................
USING ECHOLOCATION, A BAT TRAVELING AT HIGH SPEEDS CAN DETECT AN OBJECT THE WIDTH OF A HUMAN HAIR!

Bats emit bursts of high-pitched sounds to locate prey.

Echoes bounce back from a nearby moth.

It takes a bat less than half a second to capture a moth after detecting it.

ELEPHANTS

You would need a spectacular snout to breathe, drink, shower, touch, grab, and talk using only your nose. Elephants use their talented trunks to do all those things! An elephant's trunk contains more than 100,000 muscles that can lift 550 pounds (about 250 kg). Two nostrils run the length of the trunk. Elephants can suck water up their nostrils and then shoot it into their mouths—breathing through their mouths while their trunk is full. They can even use the trunk as a snorkel as they swim. They greet each other with a "trunk shake," and raise their trunks high to get a better smell of danger. Elephants are the last remaining members of a prehistoric group of plant-eating mammals that included the mammoth. Asian elephants are considered threatened, and African are endangered.

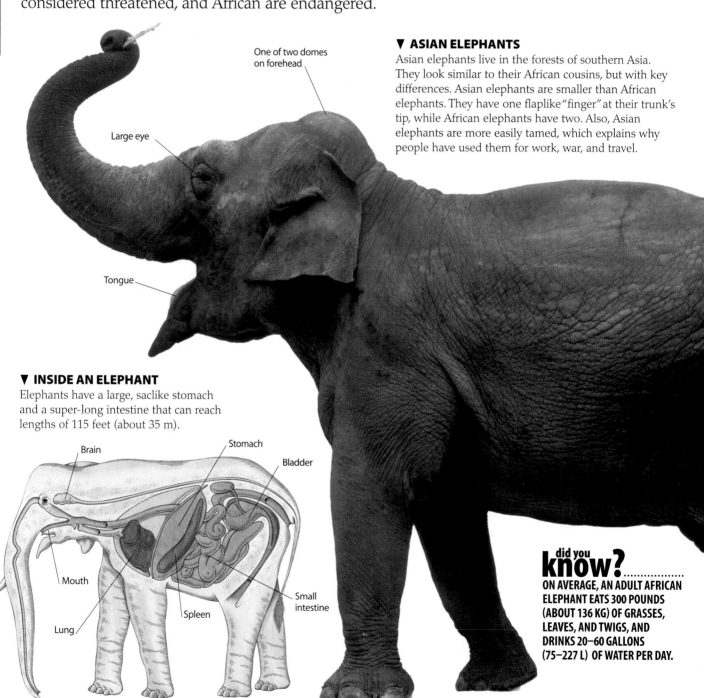

One of two domes
on forehead

Large eye

Tongue

▼ ASIAN ELEPHANTS

Asian elephants live in the forests of southern Asia. They look similar to their African cousins, but with key differences. Asian elephants are smaller than African elephants. They have one flaplike "finger" at their trunk's tip, while African elephants have two. Also, Asian elephants are more easily tamed, which explains why people have used them for work, war, and travel.

▼ INSIDE AN ELEPHANT

Elephants have a large, saclike stomach and a super-long intestine that can reach lengths of 115 feet (about 35 m).

Brain

Stomach

Bladder

Mouth

Lung

Spleen

Small
intestine

did you
know?..................
ON AVERAGE, AN ADULT AFRICAN
ELEPHANT EATS 300 POUNDS
(ABOUT 136 KG) OF GRASSES,
LEAVES, AND TWIGS, AND
DRINKS 20–60 GALLONS
(75–227 L) OF WATER PER DAY.

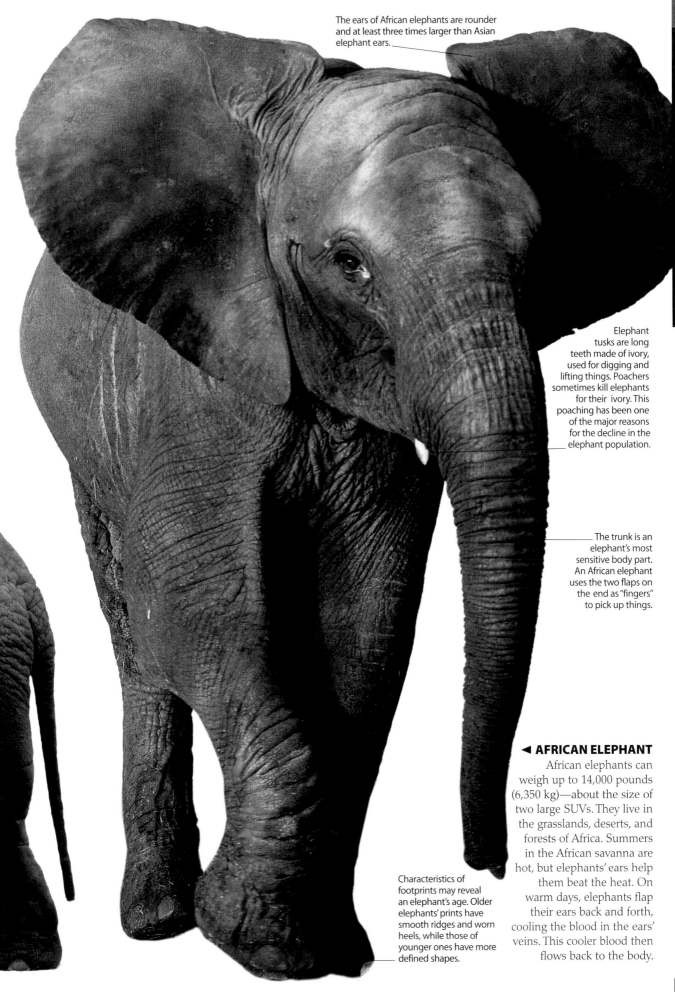

The ears of African elephants are rounder and at least three times larger than Asian elephant ears.

Elephant tusks are long teeth made of ivory, used for digging and lifting things. Poachers sometimes kill elephants for their ivory. This poaching has been one of the major reasons for the decline in the elephant population.

The trunk is an elephant's most sensitive body part. An African elephant uses the two flaps on the end as "fingers" to pick up things.

Characteristics of footprints may reveal an elephant's age. Older elephants' prints have smooth ridges and worn heels, while those of younger ones have more defined shapes.

◄ AFRICAN ELEPHANT

African elephants can weigh up to 14,000 pounds (6,350 kg)—about the size of two large SUVs. They live in the grasslands, deserts, and forests of Africa. Summers in the African savanna are hot, but elephants' ears help them beat the heat. On warm days, elephants flap their ears back and forth, cooling the blood in the ears' veins. This cooler blood then flows back to the body.

ENERGY CONSERVATION

Electrons are constantly on the move in your home. Lights, computers, air conditioners, and appliances all use electrical energy, or the energy of electrons in motion. In many homes, electrical energy also provides heat and hot water. It takes a lot of energy to power all those things. Most of this energy comes from burning nonrenewable fuels—fuels that would take Earth millions of years to make again—such as oil, natural gas, and coal. Harvesting and refining these fuels also uses energy. Burning all that fuel produces greenhouse gases. Greenhouse gases trap heat in Earth's atmosphere, which leads to global warming. To help combat global warming, you can conserve, or use less, energy. To conserve energy, you need to know which appliances use the most energy and then figure out some ways to cut back on their energy use.

A QUICK CUP ▶

Appliances are often labeled by their power, which is the units of energy they use in an hour. The units of electric power are called *watts* or *kilowatts* (1,000 watts). Electricity use is usually measured in kilowatt-hours (kWh)—the number of kilowatts used multiplied by the hours an appliance is on. This 1-kilowatt electric coffee maker, for example, uses less than 100 kWh of electricity each year—if it is turned off after 15 minutes.

If the coffee maker stays on for 8 hours every day, it uses almost 3,000 kWh of electricity each year.

Running the pump, filter, and heater uses about 260 kWh of electricity in a year.

◀ OFF AND ON

The average American household uses more than 11,000 kWh of electricity each year. How much of that could we conserve? We make choices every day. A tropical aquarium is on all the time, yet it uses less than 1 kWh of electricity in a day—less than an air conditioner uses in an *hour*. Now that's an opportunity to conserve! Keep the fish, and turn off the air conditioner when you aren't using it.

A cold-water wash plus a clothesline saves about 2,000 kWh of electricity per year!

CLEANING UP ▲

Washing and drying your clothes takes a lot of electricity. For a typical family, washing in hot water and rinsing in warm water uses about 2,184 kWh of electricity a year. Most of the electricity is used to heat the water. Washing and rinsing in cold water reduces that number to 103 kWh per year. Drying the clothes on a clothesline afterward conserves about 972 kWh per year.

did you know? ON AVERAGE, AMERICANS HAVE 45 LIGHT BULBS THROUGHOUT THE HOUSE. ....

Compact fluorescent light bulbs last 10 times longer than incandescent bulbs do.

SHEDDING A NEW LIGHT

One of the easiest ways to conserve energy is by changing a light bulb. A traditional light bulb, called an *incandescent bulb*, converts about three-fourths of its electrical energy into heat instead of light. You can feel it! A compact fluorescent bulb (CFL), on the other hand, uses only 13 watts of electricity to produce as much light as a 60-watt incandescent bulb.

EQUATOR

The equator is like a belt that circles Earth's middle. It is an imaginary line located equal distances from the North and South poles, at what is known as 0 degrees latitude. The equator is the longest line of latitude on Earth, measuring about 24,901 miles (about 40,075 km)! It is often used as a point of reference. The distance of each location from the equator determines how many hours of sunlight it receives each day and how direct that sunlight is. The areas near the equator are very, very hot! But, since other factors also affect weather, such as nearness to the ocean, mountains, height above sea level, and atmospheric conditions, temperature and rainfall in each place can vary a lot. That is why you can find both tropical rain forests and deserts near the equator.

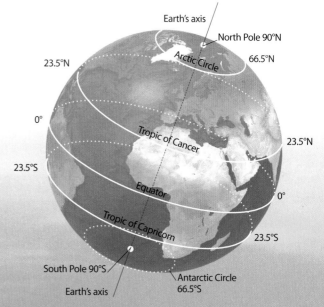

LINES OF LATITUDE ▲

Earth's axis is tilted slightly, relative to the sun. Places farther from the equator receive varying amounts of sunlight during the year, depending on which of Earth's hemispheres is facing the sun. The area near the equator, called the *tropics*, gets about 12 hours of sunlight each day year-round. The tropics lie between two other imaginary lines of latitude, the Tropic of Cancer and the Tropic of Capricorn.

Drought has lowered the level of Lake Turkana, concentrating the water's salt and other chemicals so the water is now barely drinkable.

AN AFRICAN DESERT

Many areas along the equator are parched and dry. Rainfall in this part of Kenya is typically less than 8 inches (about 200 mm) annually. Running through this desert landscape is a valley, called a *rift*, which formed as pieces of Earth's crust pulled—and continue to pull—apart. Lakes formed in these valleys. This village is on Lake Turkana, which is a large but shallow lake in the middle of a desert.

TROPICAL RAIN FOREST OF HAWAII ▶

The Hawaiian Islands lie just south of the Tropic of Cancer. The weather can vary dramatically within short distances. Honolulu can receive more than 20 inches (508 mm) of rain in a single year. Three miles inland, here in Manoa Valley, more than 150 inches (3,810 mm) fall. Like other tropical rain forests near the equator, this one is rainy, warm, and teeming with life.

did you know?
....
TANZANIA'S MOUNT KILIMANJARO IS ONLY 3 DEGREES OF LATITUDE SOUTH OF THE EQUATOR—ONLY 207 MILES (ABOUT 333 KM)—BUT ITS PEAK IS CAPPED WITH SNOW.

Acacias, or umbrella thorn trees, provide shade, food, fuel, and more for the people who live near the lake.

ERYOPS

Eryops was a salamander-like amphibian that lived nearly 270 million years ago. This was no ordinary animal. Reaching 6 feet long (1.8 m) and 200 pounds (90.7 kg), it was one amplified amphibian! Like most amphibians, Eryops lived both on land and in water. It was a powerful hunter. A swamp dweller, Eryops preyed on small reptiles, fish, and other amphibians. It lived during the Permian period, the sixth and final phase of the Paleozoic era. This geologic era featured many organisms evolving to meet the demands of life on land. Eryops disappeared about 250 million years ago during the largest extinction in Earth's history—even bigger than the one that would later kill the dinosaurs.

did you
know?..
THE PERMIAN EXTINCTION THAT WIPED OUT ERYOPS ALSO DESTROYED NEARLY EVERY TREE, 95 PERCENT OF MARINE SPECIES, AND ABOUT 70 PERCENT OF ALL LARGE LAND ANIMALS.

In Greek, the word *eryops* means "drawn-out face" and refers to the animal's long, alligator-like skull.

Unlike many species, Eryops's shoulders were not connected to its skull. This helped it move better on land.

A strong, thick backbone kept Eryops's body from collapsing beneath its own weight.

Eryops had strong jaws and sharp teeth, for grasping its prey, but it could not chew. It tossed its head up and back to swallow.

Eryops walked with short, broad strides. It used great effort to keep its massive body lifted off the ground.

Eryops's pelvis was large and muscular.

▲ A SKELETON'S STORY

Fossils from Eryops have been found in Permian-aged rocks from Texas, New Mexico, and the eastern United States. These bones and teeth have given scientists information about the evolution of Eryops from a water-dwelling fish to an air-breathing amphibian. The shape and structure of the skeleton tell a story about Eryops's life as a peak Permian predator.

An artist's drawing of what Eryops might have looked like

ESTIMATION

How many stars are there in the universe? There are too many to count one by one. Instead, you might try estimating the number of stars.

Estimation is the process of making a rough calculation of a number based on reason. Scientists use estimation when they cannot count exact numbers or take exact measurements. One way to estimate numbers is to divide a large group of objects into several equal, smaller groups, called *sample areas*, and count a representative sample. A representative sample is as much like the large group as possible, only it is small enough to count. By multiplying the exact count of the representative sample by the total number of sample areas, scientists can estimate the number of objects in the large group.

This area of the hive is almost bare. It would not make a useful representative sample because it contains many fewer bees than the rest of the hive's surface.

◄ A SWARM OF BEES
One way to estimate the number of bees on the outside of a hive is to draw a grid on a photograph of the hive. The squares on the grid must be of equal area. Imagine that a representative square in the grid contains exactly 42 bees. Then imagine that the total area of the hive is covered by 55 squares of the grid. The estimation is 42 times 55, or 2,310 bees!

Scientists estimated that this invasion of locusts in the Canary Islands in 2004 brought more than 100 million insects.

▼ AN INVASION OF LOCUSTS

Two other ways to estimate uncountable numbers are using indirect measurements and examining models. To estimate how locusts spread during an invasion, scientists use satellites to photograph the plants in an area before and after the invasion. These pictures are an indirect measurement of the damage locusts do over time as they eat the plants. Then scientists can compare this new plant damage to previous examples of plant damage. Since the amount of plant damage tells the approximate size of the locust swarm, they can then calculate how many locusts it took to cause this amount of damage. These calculations make up a mathematical model.

did you know?

BY OBSERVING AND COUNTING THE GALAXIES IN ONE STRIP OF THE SKY, SCIENTISTS ESTIMATED THAT THERE ARE 70,000 MILLION MILLION MILLION—70 SEXTILLION—STARS IN THE VISIBLE UNIVERSE.

EVERGLADES

The Everglades, in the southern part of Florida, is a vast area of wetlands. Wetlands are areas that are covered with shallow water during all or most parts of the year—like a flood that never goes away. The Everglades is unique because the water there flows slowly over the land toward the ocean in a wide sheet, rather than in narrower rivers. In the Everglades, differences in land elevation create different habitats. Marshes are shallow flooded areas where grasses grow. Sloughs (rhymes with "news") are deeper bands of faster-moving water. Hammocks are areas of higher land that rarely flood. They support hardwood trees, such as live oak, red maple, and mahogany. Estuaries form where fresh water meets and mixes with seawater, providing a home for plants and animals that tolerate salt water.

The spectacled caiman gets its name from a bony ridge that runs under and between its eyes and looks as if it is wearing glasses.

Cypress trees lose their leaves in the fall and grow new leaves in the spring.

When its jaws are closed, you cannot see the largest lower tooth of a caiman, which is visible in crocodiles.

CYPRESS SWAMPS ▲
Swamps, another type of Everglades habitat, are usually covered in water for most of the year. Cypress trees grow in swamps. These cone-bearing trees can grow separately or in patches that form small tree islands. Their roots sometimes grow "knees," bumpy structures that poke above the water. It is thought that the knees allow the plant to obtain oxygen for its root system.

Cypress trees are the most flood-tolerant kind of tree in Florida.

▼ SPECTACLED CAIMAN

Caimans live in the Everglades. Related to crocodiles and alligators, caimans are water-loving reptiles that have greenish scaly skin and long tails. Males grow to be 6–8 feet (about 1.8–2.5 m). Females are smaller, usually only about 4.5 feet (almost 1.4 m) in length. They eat fish, amphibians, birds, and other reptiles. Caimans are not native to Florida. They were originally brought as pets from places such as Colombia.

did you know?..........

THE EVERGLADES ONCE COVERED 4,000 SQUARE MILES (ALMOST 10, 360 SQ KM) IN SOUTHERN FLORIDA. NOW, IT COVERS ABOUT HALF OF THAT AREA.

EXOSKELETON

Clams, spiders, lobsters, and snails all have their own body armor, called an *exoskeleton*. These tough coverings act as protection, keeping the outside out and the inside in. They also support the creature living inside. Like our skin, these coverings help protect the animal from drying out. Unlike skin, exoskeletons do not automatically increase in size when the animal inside grows. Some animals, such as clams, are able to add onto their shells layer by layer. Insects and crustaceans such as crabs, with more complicated body shapes, have a different solution. These creatures molt, or shed, their exoskeleton regularly as they grow. Some even reabsorb or eat their old outer covering to keep the valuable proteins inside.

SINGING CICADAS ▶
Cicadas are flying insects that feed on the sap of plants. They have several different life stages, and their exoskeletons molt as the insect grows. The young nymph cicadas live underground for up to 17 years, and suck on roots for food. Once they emerge from the ground, adult cicadas mate, produce eggs, and then die—all within a few weeks.

The fiddler crab's limbs are attached to its hard shell, or *carapace*, shown here on a model of the crab. The entire exoskeleton must be molted as the crab grows.

Four pairs of limbs are used for walking and burrowing. The fifth pair is used for feeding and defense.

Cicadas are also called *dry bugs*, because they leave behind a dry shell after molting. The abandoned exoskeletons are often a sign that the cicadas have emerged from underground.

Large powerful muscles operate the top section of the claw, allowing it to open, close, and crush.

The male's single large claw is used to fight and to attract mates. It uses its small claw for feeding.

◀ GIVE HIM A BIG HAND
Female and young fiddler crabs have two front claws of the same size, but mature male fiddler crabs have one claw that is much larger than the other. This claw can be up to 65 percent of the crab's weight!

Eye stalks poke through holes in the shell.

COIL OF ARMOR ▶

This slippery common snail also has an exoskeleton, which protects its soft body. The snail's body can be squeezed into the shell when the snail is alarmed. The smallest species of snail is less than a millimeter long, but the largest land snail can reach 15 inches (almost 39 cm)—that's longer than some dogs—and is a heavyweight at almost 2 pounds (about 900 g).

A snail grows its shell by adding new layers of shell-forming calcium carbonate to the opening. It thickens its shell by adding to the inside lining.

The exoskeleton of cicadas and many crustaceans is made of chitin. Chitin is rigid except between certain body parts where it is thin enough to allow for movement

Thin, strong veins stiffen the wings. A hinge allows the cicada's wings to flap.

Most land snails have two pairs of retractable tentacles on their head. The longer pair has light-sensitive eyespots.

Many people around the world eat cicadas—especially the females because they're usually meatier. The cicada exoskeleton is also used in some traditional Chinese medicines to treat high fevers.

did you know?..........................

IF A CRAB LOSES A LIMB TO A PREDATOR, IT CAN GROW A NEW ONE! THE NEW APPENDAGE GROWS UNDER THE SHELL AND CAN BE REPLACED WITHIN A FEW MOLTS.

DO THE SIDEWAYS SCUTTLE ▼

A crab's movement is restricted by its exoskeleton, and by the way its legs bend. The joints in its appendages can move forward and back in only one direction—the way our knees move—but their "knees" face sideways. As a result, most crabs move only sideways. A crab can tuck its limbs in tightly, allowing it to squeeze into small areas, avoiding fish or larger crabs who may want a snack.

The sharp ends of the crab's legs can grip irregular surfaces.

Jointed limbs bend in one direction only.

EXTINCTION

Imagine an asteroid the size of Manhattan hurtling toward Earth, its edges in flames as it burns through the atmosphere. If you think such an event happens only in science fiction, think again. Scientists have found evidence that large asteroids have hit Earth in the past. Many hypothesize that this kind of event caused the mass extinction of the dinosaurs. Extinction happens when an entire species dies out. A mass extinction occurs when hundreds of different species become extinct in a single event. The largest mass extinction took place about 250 million years ago, just before the first dinosaurs came into existence. This event, called the *Permian–Triassic extinction,* killed off more than 90 percent of all sea life and 70 percent of land animals.

▼ CAUSES OF MASS EXTINCTION

At least five mass extinctions have taken place in the last 540 million years. These may have been caused by asteroids or comets colliding with Earth, increased volcanic activity, ice ages, or changes in sea level. Species that survive have a new chance at life. After the Permian-Triassic extinction, new species took the places of those that disappeared. Dinosaurs, such as *Corythosaurus* and *Ceratops,* dominated the era that followed.

Plant-eating *Corythosaurus* had a toothless bill like a duck and was 30 feet (about 9 m) long.

Members of the *Ceratops* genus had beaklike mouths and bony frills on their heads. Some had horns. They probably ate plants.

The asteroid believed to have caused the dinosaur extinction created a crater that is about 112 miles (180 km) in diameter in Mexico's Yucatán Peninsula.

did you know?..
AN ENDANGERED SPECIES IS DEFINED AS ONE THAT IS IN DANGER OF EXTINCTION THROUGHOUT ALL OR A SIGNIFICANT PORTION OF ITS RANGE.

◄ SURVIVING AN ASTEROID COLLISION

Species that survive an asteroid collision confront other problems. Dust sent up when the asteroid hits Earth could darken the sky for weeks. The dust can strain breathing, harm plants that depend on sunlight, and kill single-celled organisms that are sensitive to even subtle chemical changes in their surroundings. The extinction of some species can cause the death of others that depend on them for food and oxygen.

Tyrannosaurus bones found in the Rocky Mountain region of North America show bite marks made by *T. rex* teeth, leading scientists to believe they fought one another or were cannibals.

Scientists believe that *T. Rex* was wiped out during the Cretaceous-Tertiary mass extinction, which may have been caused by the Yucatán Peninsula asteroid.

▲ WAS *T. REX* IN YOUR BACK YARD?

Not all extinction hypotheses can be proved, leaving scientists with incomplete answers. Fossils provide the strongest evidence of extinction. Scientists have also observed a pattern in fossils that suggests mass extinctions occur every 26–30 million years. Some believe the pattern relates to regular travel paths of asteroids and other celestial objects.

EYE SCAN

No two eyes are alike. Even your left eye and right eye are different from one another. Eye-scanning technologies take advantage of unique patterns in the eye for identification, much the way fingerprints do. Eye scans and fingerprints are both forms of biometrics, measurement techniques that use physical characteristics to identify people. Some physical characteristics, such as height and weight, change over time. Certain features of your eyes, though, remain constant. There are two kinds of eye scans. Iris scans measure the unique pattern of the iris, the colored part around the pupil. Retinal scans measure the pattern of blood vessels on the retina, the lining at the back of the inside of the eyeball. Iris scans are easier to use and therefore are more popular. However, both kinds of eye scans are considered the most accurate forms of biometric identification available.

WHAT HAPPENS IN AN IRIS EYE SCAN? ▶
First, a camera takes a picture of the eye. A computer locates the iris and searches for special features. Next, the computer creates a record of the iris pattern. When a new scan is taken, the computer compares it with the recorded iris patterns to find a match. More than 200 features are used to verify the match. The entire process takes only a few seconds.

This woman stands so she can see her eye's reflection in the scanning device.

SCHOOL SCAN ▲
This school in New Jersey uses iris-scanning technology to protect students. Only authorized adults—those whose irises are recognized—can enter the school. Eye-scanning technologies are gaining in popularity. They are used to identify prisoners, airport travelers, and bank customers. They also secure military facilities, power plants, and some hotels.

The device's computer divides the iris image into many areas and looks for unique features in each.

The device uses binary code, a computer language made of 0's and 1's, to describe the iris pattern.

Iris-scanning technology, patented in 1994, uses a complex process to record and recognize its features. The iris has ridges and furrows as a fingerprint does. It may also have freckles, which are spots of pigment on the iris.

did you know?............
THE CHANCE OF AN IRIS SCAN BEING WRONG IS ABOUT ONE IN ONE MILLION!

FAMILY TREE

Meet the Felidae family, better known as cats or felines. They range from lions and tigers to domestic cats that you might have as a pet. The first cat ancestors evolved about 37 million years ago. The family tree branches into smaller groups, called *subfamilies*. Most of the cats that you know are in the Felinae subfamily. The big cats, such as lions, form the Pantherinae subfamily, and the cheetah is in a unique subfamily of cats that don't climb. Cats are native to every continent except Australia and Antarctica. Depending on where they lived, cats developed adaptations, or special features, to help them survive in their particular environments. Each subfamily is broken down into smaller groups, called *genera* (singular: genus). Each genus is made up of different species. These days, the Felidae family consists of about 37 species of living cats. While each species has its own characteristics, all the family members share many common features. Let's look in on a small family reunion.

Tigers are the only kind of cat with striped fur, which provides camouflage in the tall grasses and forests where they hide.

Servals have the biggest ears of any member of the cat family relative to their body size.

▲ LONG LEGS, BIG EARS

The serval, with its long legs and big ears, lives in the grasslands and brush of Africa. It's a member of the Felinae subfamily and the only cat in its genus. The serval is usually about 20 inches (about 50 cm) high at the shoulder and weighs about 33 pounds (almost 15 kg). It is especially adept at leaping and landing on prey such as hares, quail, frogs, and flamingos.

Most members of the cat family have long tails, helping them balance when they run and jump.

did you know?..............................
THE BIGGEST CAT OF ALL WAS BRED IN CAPTIVITY FROM A TIGER MOTHER AND A LION FATHER. "LIGERS" CAN GROW TO TWICE THE SIZE OF A NORMAL TIGER.

DENTAL DIVERGENCE ▶

There are some extinct members of the cat family, such as the *Smilodon*, a type of saber-toothed cat. About 20 million years ago, the cat family split into two groups. One led to modern cats and the other led to these now extinct saber-toothed cats.

These 7-inch (almost 18-cm) teeth were probably used on large prey, such as mastodons, whose extinction coincided with the that of the *Smilodon*.

Cats' ears can move independently, helping the animal locate the direction of sounds.

◀ CATS THAT ROAR

Tigers are the largest members of the cat family. They are part of the *Panthera* genus of big, roaring cats, which includes lions, leopards, and jaguars. Different species of tigers have adapted to life in places as different as the Siberian tundra and Indonesia's tropical forests. Their numbers in the wild have dwindled, though, from about 100,000 in 1800 to fewer than 5,000 today, making tigers an endangered species.

All cats can hiss, spit, and growl. Big cats have special cartilage supporting their tongues that allows them to roar.

▼ WILDCATS

Domestic cats, such as this brown tabby, are descended from *Felis silvestris*, a species of small wildcat native to Europe, Asia, and Africa. Scientists believe that around 10,000 years ago, a wildcat became friendly with people in a Middle Eastern settlement. The cat may have helped get rid of small rodents that ate their grain. Over time, these wildcats adapted to living with people, and their descendants became modern domestic cats.

Cats' tongues are covered with sharp projections that slant backwards, helping the cat scrape meat from the bones of prey and lap water backward into their mouths.

Cats' front feet have five toes and their hind feet have four. Each foot has sharp claws. Most cats' claws—except the cheetah's—can be drawn in, or retracted.

Cats are called *digitigrades*, which means that they walk on their toes with the back part of their feet raised.

FARMING

Picture a farm: a red barn with a tall silo, a farmer on a tractor, chickens in the yard. That's one type of farm, but most of the food we eat comes from industrial-sized farms that cover thousands of acres. Equipment that can seed and harvest huge tracts of land, fertilizers and pesticides that can increase crop yields, and new technology for processing plants and animals into food have made farms much more productive. Yet that success has come at a cost. Today's huge farms rely heavily on fossil fuels, produce greenhouse gases, strain water resources, and often only grow single crops, such as corn. Single crops are more vulnerable to insects and can deplete the soil, so they require more pesticides and fertilizers. Farming is complex business. On the one hand, farmers need to produce as much food as possible to feed growing numbers of people throughout the world. On the other hand, farmers need to farm in ways that protect and sustain the land, water, plants, and animals that provide our food now so that they can continue to do so in the future. A growing movement to support small, local farms has made fresh food, often grown with fewer chemicals and recently harvested, available to more people.

EGG FARMING ▲
About 340 million hens lay almost 90 billion eggs per year in the United States. Most come from chickens housed in long rows of crowded cages. Some egg producers are trying a different method: feeding chickens only organic feed and letting them run around.

DOWN ON THE SALMON FARM ▲

Almost half of the fish people consume comes from fish farming, a worldwide industry. Scientists are working to find ways to raise healthy fish without harming the environment.

AMBER WAVES OF KELP ▶

The huge algae, or seaweed, called *kelp*, grows in forests in cold ocean water. Kelp is used in foods, medicine, and fertilizer. Kelp farmers have had some success planting stands of kelp, but it can be difficult because sea urchins eat the seedlings. The goal of those exploring kelp farming is to provide a sustainable food source and produce the basic ingredient for some biofuels.

Machines such as this combine harvest more than 2 billion bushels of wheat each year in the United States.

did you know?

IN 1950, ONE U.S. FARMER COULD FEED 15 PEOPLE. BY 1995, ONE FARMER COULD FEED 128 PEOPLE, 34 OF WHOM LIVED OUTSIDE THE UNITED STATES.

DK EDUCATION

Design Miranda Brown and Ali Scrivens, The Book Makers
Managing Art Editor Richard Czapnik
Design Director Stuart Jackman
Publisher Sophie Mitchell

PEARSON

The people who made up the **DK Big Ideas of Science Reference Library** team—representing digital product development, editorial, editorial services, manufacturing, and production—are listed below.

Johanna Burke, Jessica Chase, Arthur Ciccone, Amanda Ferguson, Kathryn Fobert, Christian Henry, Sharon Inglis, Russ Lappa, Dotti Marshall, Robyn Matzke, Tim McDonald, Maria Milczarek, Célio Pedrosa, Stephanie Rogers, Logan Schmidt, Christine Whitney

CREDITS

The publisher would like to thank the following for their kind permission to reproduce their photographs:

Key: t-top; b-below/bottom; c-center; l-left; r-right

Cover and i) Getty Images: Romilly Lockyer and Zac Macaulay (crash-dummy montage); Shutterstock, Inc.: CJPhoto (lettering). **ii–iii)** Dorling Kindersley: NIKID Design Ltd. **iv–v)** Dorling Kindersley: Combustion. **vi)** Dorling Kindersley: Royal British Columbia Museum, Victoria, Canada. **vii)** Corbis: Jim Reed (b); NASA: ESA/The Hubble Heritage Team/STScI/AURA (tr). **viii)** Science Photo Library: Pasieka. **x–xi)** NASA. **2–3** Dorling Kindersley: Combustion. **3** Corbis: Visuals Unlimited (br). **5** Dorling Kindersley: NASA (tr). **6–7** Corbis: P. Deliss/Godong. **8** Corbis: Gabe Palmer (bl). **8–9** Corbis: Michael Barley. **10–11** Corbis: Jonathan Blair. **12** Corbis: Phil Schermeister (bl). **12–13** Getty Images: Romilly Lockyer. **13** Corbis: David Woods (br). **16–17** Corbis: Bernard Annebicque/Sygma. **18–19** Corbis: John McAnulty. **21** Science Photo Library: Omikron (tr). **22–23** Science Photo Library: Dan Schechter. **23** NASA: JPL-Caltech/R. Hurt (tr). **24–25** Dorling Kindersley: NIKID Design Ltd. **26–27** NASA: Matthew Spinelli. **28** Getty Images: Art Wolfe (cl). **28–29** Corbis: Frans Lanting. **32–33** NHPA/Photoshot: Danny Green. **33** Corbis: Tony Wilson-Bligh/Papillo (tr). **34–35** Dorling Kindersley: Index Stock/Alamy. **36–37** Corbis: Robert Llewellyn/Zefa. **38–39** National Geographic Stock: Greg Marshall. **39** Corbis: Momatiuk-Eastcott (tr). **41** Dorling Kindersley: Natural History Museum, London (bc, br). **43** Science Photo Library: James King-Holmes (tr). **44–45** Corbis: Ralph White. **45** Corbis: Ralph White (tr). **46** Science Photo Library: Michael Donne. **46–47** Science Photo Library: L. Steinmark/Custom Medical Stock Photo. **47** Corbis: Paul Seheult/Eye Ubiquitous (tr). **50–51** Fujifilm UK. **52** Dorling Kindersley: Royal Tyrrell Museum of Paleontology, Alberta, Canada (bl). **52–53** Dorling Kindersley: Jonathan Hateley, model maker. **56** Corbis: Visuals Unlimited (bl). **56–57** Science Photo Library: TEK Image. **58** Dorling Kindersley: Natural History Museum, London (br). **58–59** Corbis: Stuart Westmorland. **60–61** Corbis: Jim Reed. **61** Corbis: Jim Reed (tl). **62** Corbis: Gene Blevins (bl). **62–63** Corbis: Chris Williams/Icon SMI. **64–65** Lifestraw. **68–69** Corbis: Peter Lillie/Gallo Images. **70–71** NASA: Goddard Space Flight Center Scientific Visualization Studio. **72** Dorling Kindersley: Peter Griffiths, model maker (c); Getty Images (br). **72–73** Corbis: Reuters/Kimimasa Mayama. **74** NASA: SOHO/ESA (bl). **76–77** Dorling Kindersley: Oxford Scientific Films. **81** Corbis: Michael Robinson/Beateworks (tc). **82–83** Corbis: Andy Aitchison. **85** Dorling Kindersley: Natural History Museum, London (tc). **86** Corbis: Sheldan Collins (l). **86–87** Corbis: Juan Medina/Reuters. **90–91** Dorling Kindersley: Booth Museum of Natural History, Brighton. **92–93** Corbis: Reuters. **93** Dorling Kindersley: Graham High at Centaur Studios (r). **94** Getty Images (bl). **94–95** Science Photo Library: Pasieka. **97** Dorling Kindersley: Natural History Museum, London (tr). **98–99** Corbis: Terry W. Eggers.

All other images © Dorling Kindersley
For further information see: www.dkimages.com